The Gigli Concert

'One of the greatest Irish plays of the century.' *Irish Times*

'Murphy's words waltz through the auditorium in musical waves . . . a fabulous piece.' *Irish Press*

'The play is a mighty entertainment . . . It is a flamboyant all-enveloping swirling cloak of a play rather than a made-to-measure strait-jacket.' *Sunday Independent*

'This is a wonderful, wonderful play, the jewel in Murphy's career to date, the like of which one is rarely privileged to see.' *Sunday Business Post*

This new version of **The Gigli Concert** opened at the Abbey Theatre, Dublin in March 1991 to great critical acclaim. JPW King is a quack psychologist who helps people reach their potential for greatness. One day a client arrives needing his help – an Irish millionaire who wants to sing like Gigli . . .

Tom Murphy's work includes the internationally acclaimed *A Whistle in the Dark* (Theatre Royal, Stratford East, 1961, Long Wharf Theatre, New Haven, Connecticut and New York; Royal Court, London 1989), *Famine* (Peacock Theatre, Dublin, 1968, Royal Court, London 1969), *Bailegangaire* (Druid Theatre Company, Galway, 1985, Donmar Warehouse, London 1986, BBC Radio 1987) winner of the Harvey's Best Play Award and the Sunday Tribune Theatre Award 1985–6, *Too Late for Logic* (Abbey Theatre, Dublin, 1989) and *The Patriot Game* (Peacock Theatre, Dublin, 1991). He was born in Tuam, County Galway. During the sixties he lived in London and now lives in Dublin. He is a member of Aosdá

Tom Murphy

The Gigli Concert

Methuen Drama

A Methuen Modern Play

First published in Great Britain in 1988 by Methuen London in
After Tragedy. This revised edition published in 1991
by Methuen Drama, Michelin House, 81 Fulham Road, London SW3 6RB
and distributed in the United States of America by HEB. Inc, 361 Hanover
Street, Portsmouth, New Hampshire 03801 3959.

A CIP catalogue record for this book is available
from the British Library

ISBN 0-413-65930-5

Typeset by Hewer Text Composition Services, Edinburgh
Printed and bound in Great Britain
by Cox & Wyman Ltd, Cardiff Road, Reading

*The photograph on the front cover is of Beniamino Gigli and is
reproduced by kind permission of the Metropolitan Opera Archive, New York.
The photograph of Tom Murphy on the back cover is by Fergus Bourke.*

Caution

For Bennan

The Gigli Concert was first performed at the Abbey Theatre, Dublin on Thursday, 29 September 1983 with the following cast:

JPW King	Tom Hickey
Irish Man	Godfrey Quigley
Mona	Kate Flynn

Directed by	Patrick Mason
Designed by	Bronwen Casson with Frank Hallinan Flood
Lighting by	Tony Wakefield

This new version of **The Gigli Concert** was first performed on Tuesday, 19 March 1991 at the Abbey Theatre, Dublin with the following cast:

JPW King	Tom Hickey
Irish Man	Tony Doyle
Mona	Ingrid Craigie

Directed by	Patrick Mason
Designed by	Monica Frawley
Lighting by	Tony Wakefield

The action is set in JPW King's office which is also his living quarters.

Note

The aria 'Tu che a Dio spiegasti l'ali' on page 75 is the Pearl recording with Gigli, bass and chorus; the same aria on page 85 is a different Pearl recording: Gigli, solo voice (without bass and chorus). The **Irish Man**'s 'Ida' story, pages 53–5, is embraced by 'Toselli's Serenade'. In the trio from 'Attila' – 'Tu sol quest anima' – page 81, the opening soprano solo is to be associated with **Mona**, the tenor solo with **JPW**'s action, and the following bass solo to be timed with **Irish Man**'s entrance and associated with his action.

Scene One

*Beniamino Gigli's voice singing 'O Paradiso' has introduced the play;
it continues for some moments into Scene One, diminishing, and becomes
lost, eventually.*

*A table lamp with a red shade, switched on, and a shaft of yellow light
from the washroom, off.* **JPW** *comes out of the washroom and goes to
his desk. His appearance complements his dingy surroundings (not
yet clearly defined). He is English, upper-middle-class, tempering his
accent at times with an Irish intonation and some Irishisms.*

*He is scraping the remains of a pot of jam on to a piece of bread, then
washing it down – his breakfast – with a careful measure from the
remains of a bottle of vodka. He interrupts this business to make some
illegal adjustment to the telephone connection-box on the wall, then his
intense concentration rapping out a number on his telephone with the
edge of his hand. (His rapping is illegal phone-tapping: all this a
recurring action when he wants to use the phone.) His vulnerability,
waiting, holding his breath.*

JPW Me . . . Fine . . . Is it? . . . Yes usually sunny after . . .
Yes, and crisp . . . after frost . . . No, I'm still here . . . Same
answer I suppose? (*Silently.*) Please . . . (*He nods solemnly
to her reply.*) . . . 'Bye . . . What? . . . No, I shan't phone you
again . . . I promise . . . I promise . . . 'Bye.

*He goes to the window and lets up the blind. Morning light into the
room defining the set. Faded lettering on the street-side of the window
'JPW KING – DYNAMATOLOGIST'. He stands looking out over
the roofs of the city.*

Christ, how am I going to get through today?

*The office is dingy. A bed that converts into a couch, a desk with a
telephone, a kettle, filing cabinet, clothes about the place, books, dusty*

charts on a wall and a photograph of 'Steve', another wall and door in frosted-glass panels, flowers withering in a vase, an old leather bag (suitcase) . . .

A ring of a bell on an outer door. A second and third ring. **JPW** *becoming wary. Into action: readjustment to telephone connection-box. Outer door opening and the silhouette of an* **Irish Man** *in the next room, outside the frosted-glass panels.* **Irish Man** *knocking at door.*

JPW Yes? . . . Who is it?

Irish Man Mr King?

JPW Who is it? Who is that?

Irish Man Can I come in?

JPW Pardon?

Irish Man To talk.

JPW To? . . . To what?

Irish Man (*muffled*) To sing.

JPW What did you say? . . . What did he say? To what? . . . Hello? Hello? . . . Bloody hell.

Breakfast things into drawers, bed reconverted to couch, too late to shave, but spectacles from somewhere for effect. He unlocks the glass-panelled door which leads to an anteroom.

Yes?

Irish Man Mr King?

JPW What?

Irish Man Can I come in?

JPW What do you want?

Irish Man Ah . . . (*He comes in.*)

JPW There is possibly some mistake, Mr – Mr. (*Off, a church clock chiming the half hour.*) What time is it? Half-twelve?

Irish Man Eleven.

JPW I must get the lock on that (*Outer.*) door mended.

The **Irish Man**, *though with head bowed, is taking in the dingy room.* **JPW** *assessing* **Irish Man**: *the expensive respectable dress, top coat, silk scarf, gloves, hat (hat a little out of keeping: 30s–40s American style – as worn by Gigli) and* **Irish Man**'s *hand in his pocket, quietly toying with something – a recurring action – it could be a gun.*

Irish Man I . . .

JPW Yes.

Irish Man . . . happened to see your sign as I was passing.

JPW What sign?

Irish Man Are you the? (*He nods at the lettering on the window.*)

JPW Dynamatologist.

Irish Man JPW King.

JPW I have the letters before my name.

Irish Man You were letting up the blind.

JPW Well, actually, I have been meaning to have that sign – removed?

Irish Man I read something about you.

JPW Me?

Irish Man Your organisation.

JPW Anything good?

Irish Man Well, it was a few years ago. In the papers.

JPW Personally, I thought that article a bit unfair myself. Hmm?

Irish Man *nods*.

I mean to say, water off my back as far as I am . . . You have not come about? (*The telephone.*) Have you come to consult me?

Irish Man *considering* **JPW**.

I mean to say . . .

Irish Man Yes. (*Or an ambiguous nod.*)

JPW Well, that's different. Yes, if you would care to? (*Sit.*) As you please. But lest there should be some misunderstanding, I should say at the outset that dynamatology is not a military oriented movement. Self-realisation, you know? Because I had another caller, a gentleman of enquiring intellect, undoubtedly, yes, but had misinterpreted our meaning, in a trench-coat. Hmm? (**Irish Man** *nods.*) I knew that. As Steve puts it, mind is the essence of being alive. Steve, our founder and leader. Revolutionary thinker.

Irish Man It said in the papers –

JPW Water off my back: wanting us banned in Britain.

Irish Man About ye saying anything is possible.

JPW That is what I am explaining. The emphasis they put on the brain. But what is brain? Biological matter, meat. Mind is the essence. Yes?

Irish Man I haven't much time for philosophy.

JPW Busy man, aren't we all.

Irish Man No, I've all the time in the world – if I want it.

JPW Check. Your simple notion of life as substance is useful, I dare say, but we have gone beyond the macroscopic level into the subatomic world, and substance is simply – nonsense. Atoms, my friend. Atoms consist of whirlings – you may call them particles but we call them whirlings – and whirlings are not made of – anything. But what are our whirlings presently doing? In layman's terms, dancing with each other, and that is an awful waste of energy. So what are we to do? Process of destratification until we arrive at that state we call Nihil where we can start putting our little dancers to proper work, and working properly they can go a very long way indeed to project you beyond the boundaries that are presently limiting you. Now you have a question.

Irish Man How much?

JPW Pardon?

Irish Man Your fees.

JPW Fees can wait. *The* priority, a good relationship of trust, mutual feed of energy between auditor – that's me – and subject. Okay?

Irish Man I like to know where I stand.

JPW Ten guineas a session – that's for six. But fifteen for the first in case it is going to be the only one. That was frankly put.

Irish Man That's not too bad.

JPW Do you think so?

Irish Man It's fine.

JPW Well, that was a good start. Well now, could we begin with your name?

Irish Man Rather not.

JPW That's good!

Irish Man If you don't mind.

JPW Your name! For God's sake, Mr – Mr, where has the orthodox route taken them? Into their very own not-very-pleasant strait-jackets. My style – as you have been observing – is casual.

Irish Man I haven't much time for psychiatrists – psychologists.

JPW Candid opinion? Intellectual philistines. Conflicting approaches, contradictory schools. And Freud! Now it transpires it was all about his having it off with his sister-in-law. Did you read about that? In the papers.

Irish Man My wife wanted me to see a psychologist. Our doctor wanted me to see a psychiatrist, I told them the same thing.

JPW What thing?

Irish Man That I know more about life than the lot of them put together.

JPW I see. So you chose me?

Irish Man *considering* **JPW**.

Actually this stubble is going to be a beard.

Irish Man You're a stranger here, Mr King?

JPW Well, I have been here for nearly – five years? I mean to say.

Irish Man But you're a stranger, you're English?

JPW Yes, yes, but a Tipperary grandmother. That's where I get it from. God rest her.

Irish Man Public school? (*Boarding school.*)

JPW Yes.

Irish Man I'm a self-made man.

JPW I gathered that – I mean, and aren't you proud of it!

Irish Man But not university?

JPW No, I broke my father's heart instead. But I got the trust money – eventually – (*Laughs again.*) And blew it! But that's enough about me, what do you think of me? Joke. Yes, well, time to start getting down to those old levels of data. We have no name, good. Address? No address, quite in order in my book. Telephone – in case? No. Fine. Age?

Irish Man Fifty-one.

JPW Ah! That rules out a few things, what? Yes, well. Are there many people of your acquaintance dying at the moment?

Irish Man (*rising*) I think . . .

JPW We're doing fine.

Irish Man I think we may have made a mistake.

JPW	Absolutely fine! –
Irish Man	I'll maybe call some other time –
JPW	You came to consult me –
Irish Man	No, I –
JPW	For my help –
Irish Man	I don't know what I'm doing here –
JPW	That's what I'm here for! Please –

Irish Man I don't need help! (*Hand in his pocket.*) I've got the answer! Can't talk to anyone! I'm not insane!

JPW I'm insane! I am insane. There, you nearly laughed.

Irish Man I didn't!

JPW I'm insane.

Irish Man That's your problem.

JPW I'm joking. That is what my father used to say, the boy is a dreamer, he used to say, he's crazy. Strike root was his phrase. Sit down, my friend. Mama, of course, was a different kettle of fish: the inner world, and a little poetry. What was your mother like?

Irish Man (*rounds on him*) Is it information you're looking for?!

JPW Or pace if you wish, yes, but, good heavens, if we cannot, two grown men, help one another. I mean to say do you think mental health means normal adjustment?

Irish Man I don't want normal adjustment.

JPW Exactly! Where is the achievement in standardised activity or routine trivia? Change your car, grow a carrot? I have to watch it myself, now that I have taken root. For God's sake, we might as well go back to Galileo Galilei, I say to my Helen.

Irish Man I wouldn't call building more than a thousand houses routine trivia.

JPW The house-proud life she would have me lead!

Irish Man Apart from a thousand other deals.

JPW So, you are a builder, a developer?

Irish Man An 'operator'.

JPW Got it. You have come to a standstill, you are looking for the will, the driveness to build a thousand more.

Irish Man I don't want to build anything more. This – something – cloud has come down on me.

JPW Has it happened before, is there a pattern?

Irish Man I just felt I'd like an explanation.

JPW Check. But no pattern?

Irish Man I don't mind pain. I could always – and I still can – and I've a bad back – mix concrete shovel for shovel with any navvy if a machine broke down. But this other thing. I don't understand it.

JPW No pattern. Anything else?

Irish Man What?

JPW When you were outside the door I thought you said –

Irish Man No, nothing else! How much did you say? (*Preparing to go.*)

JPW You just want an explanation –

Irish Man Ten, fifteen pounds? –

JPW You stated it as a fact.

Irish Man There's too many facts in the world. Them houses were built out of facts: corruption, brutality, backhanding, fronthanding, backstabbing, lump labour and a bit of technology.

JPW I should not have thought you the type.

Irish Man Aaw! aren't yeh good? Oh, out there, boy, you learn how to take the main chance.

JPW You don't have to pay me now. Your problem is –

Irish Man Forget it. I have it here somewhere. Ten, eleven, fourteen . . .

JPW (*watching him make up the money with notes and coins*) . . . No, you forget it.

Irish Man (*he sees* **JPW**'s *offence; he laughs harshly, shortly*) *My* problem is. Yeh, I didn't think you were such a funny man when I saw you standing in the window.

JPW Your problem is not just a problem of life, life is the problem.

Irish Man Out of a book? (*Puts money on desk.*) Fifteen pounds: fact.

JPW Thank you. I owe you ten or fifteen minutes if you have no place else to go, and I do not think you have.

Irish Man What would you like to talk about? You?

JPW Anything you like.

Irish Man . . . D'yeh like me hat? . . . I've come to a standstill. I was never a great one to talk much. Now I'd prefer to walk a mile in the other direction than say how yeh or fuck yeh to anyone. In the mornings I say Christ how am I going to get through today. The house is silent though there's a child in it. We were blessed with a late child. But I always managed to keep obscenities out of the house until lately. Now they're the only things that break the silence. Last week I was walking in the wood and my hat blew into the stream. No, not this one. (*Hat.*)

JPW You own a stream?

Irish Man I kept trying to fish it out, but it kept on escaping. So I started to shout. Obscenities. The wife come running. Her concern. Love, love, are you all right. Love. I don't want her concern. She's so – good. And I'm sure I hadn't opened my mouth to her in a month. I shouted! I'm entitled to my fucking moods. She was perplexed. Hah? I seen her age before my eyes. Then she walked away, like an old woman, through the trees. Beech. D'yeh know what a slashhook is?

JPW Like a sickle.

Irish Man Yeh. With a long shaft and more lethal. Last night I decided I'd deal with the itinerants. I'd took a couple of sleeping pills, some wine, but I knew I was in for another night with my – music. (*Short, harsh laugh.*)

JPW What pills?

Irish Man Mandrax.

JPW They've been taken off the market.

Irish Man (*ignores/dismisses this*) So, I decided I'd deal with the itinerants. The place is a shithouse, it's everywhere. Why did they choose me, my territory? And I know the doorsteps where it belongs. So. Went out. To kill them. But someone – the wife – had called the police, and they stopped me. I would've killed them otherwise. No question about that. Jail – hospital mean nothing to me. Jail – hospital have a certain appeal. Then I listened to the record for the rest of the night.

JPW The police?

Irish Man (*ignores/dismisses police*) This morning, then, the talks and whispers about psychiatrists – psychologists and their philosophy. (*Off, church clock chiming twelve.*) Time up?

JPW No!

Irish Man My – outbursts – are taking me by surprise. I don't know where the next one will lead me.

JPW Yes! I mean to say, for a time, I started to play with the traffic. I mean, the startling thing, deliberately. Like a stiff-necked toreador in streets of highly dangerous traffic! I may have been a bull-fighter in a past life.

Irish Man I want to sing.

JPW (*at the window*) Where are they all going? But all in my past needless to say, now that I have found my Helen.

Irish Man I want to sing.

JPW (*continues absently*) That's one way of putting it.

Irish Man I want to sing.

JPW That's what I thought you said out there earlier.

Irish Man Like Gigli. He was a tenor.

JPW Why not Caruso?

Irish Man It's Gigli.

JPW Ah, we must not aim too high.

Irish Man (*sharply*) I've read one or two bits of snob things about Gigli.

JPW I agree. He was emotional, was he?

Irish Man Caruso is another thing.

JPW Check. You want to sing, like Gigli, inverted commas.

Irish Man No inverted commas.

JPW Cut inverted commas, how much do you drink?

Irish Man You don't understand.

JPW Oh, I understand –

Irish Man Drink is not –

JPW Excuse me! I marked your grandiose remark, 'I know more about life than the lot of them put together'. What is that, and what is it indicative of? It is the statement of an alcoholic, my friend.

Irish Man Drink is not a problem to me!

JPW Exactly! Increase in alcohol tolerance. Excuse me!
Inability to discuss problem, grandiose statements and
aggressive behaviour – memory blackouts? – unreasonable
resentments, physical deterioration – loss of weight? – vague
spiritual desires – nearly finished – inability to initiate action –
Enough? Alibis exhausted, defeat admitted? Desire for recovery
– How much do you drink?

Irish Man I'm – a – very – poor – drinker, Mr King.

JPW Wine and those sleeping pills, lethal. People in America
jumping out of windows on wings of Mandrax.

Irish Man Drink has nothing to –

JPW I'm sorry – I enjoy a challenge, and this is a challenging
one – but – But! – if we are to get to our objective, to sing,
we have enough layers to destratify without being hampered
by toxic liquids, so all drink out! Give it a try? – Good man.
Now, tell me everything . . . Except your name.

Irish Man *toys with his hat for a moment.*

Yes, it becomes you. Place, time, date of birth is always a
good starting point.

Irish Man I was born with a voice and little else.

JPW Naked we came into the world.

Irish Man We were very poor.

JPW What did your father do?

Irish Man A cobbler.

JPW Making or mending them? It could be significant.

Irish Man He started by making them but factory-made shoes
soon put paid to that.

JPW Where was this?

Irish Man Recanati.

JPW Recan?

Irish Man Ati.

JPW What county is that in?

Irish Man Recanati is in Italy.

JPW Italian born?

Irish Man My hair was a lot darker some years ago.

JPW And your height.

Irish Man Yeh.

JPW And your frame. Quite Italianate.

Irish Man And quite in the shape of a tenor's frame.

JPW I can see that now.

Irish Man I read it somewhere, tenors tend to be short and round for glandular reasons.

JPW Interesting biological detail.

Irish Man While for bassos – basses – they tend to be tall and thin – the same law applies but only in reverse.

JPW Yes?

Irish Man It seems that only baritones are in the happy position of being normal.

JPW And, since the tenor usually plays the hero, this arrangement is all rather unfortunate.

Irish Man Yeh.

JPW What's your star?

Irish Man Star!

JPW Where exactly is Recan – ?

Irish Man Ati.

JPW Small town? – Me too – But yes?

Irish Man Sing us a song-a, Benimillo, the people used to say. I knew all the pop songs and, as you know, all the famous arias are part of our – our culture.

JPW Got your first name.

Irish Man It was a pet name.

JPW Benimillo.

Irish Man I wasn't a great boy soprano but I was the best around. Another thing I read, the really good alto boy sopranos tend to develop later as bassos or baritones, so not being that alto – although good – I had it there as well.

JPW As an indication that your future was to be a tenor. The clouds are beginning to clear at last, Benimillo.

Irish Man I sang in the choir, of course.

JPW Me too.

Irish Man But this was a fine choir and we sang, oh, Gregorian Chant and, oh, all sorts of things like the sacred music of Rossini and Gounod.

JPW Thieving Magpie.

Irish Man The singing master treated me very affectionately.

JPW Yes, a queer bird the cuckoo, he sits in the grass, his wings neatly folded, his beak up his – go on. (*He finishes a drink behind* **Irish Man**'s *back.*)

Irish Man I was taken out of class at the age of nine to sing with the twelve, fourteen-year-olds.

JPW Aha! What time is it?

Irish Man Quarter past twelve. We gave concerts.

JPW You sang solo.

Irish Man Short pieces. And sometimes we even got paid.

JPW When did your voice break?

Irish Man I was fifteen but –

JPW Good! Well, let's see what we have now.

Irish Man But my voice hadn't broke. And then, one day, these three young men came all the way from Macerata, and all because of me.

JPW What did they want?

Irish Man They wanted me to dress up as a girl and sing the soprano role in an operetta, 'Angelica's Elopement'.

JPW Strangers?

Irish Man No. But such a thing was out of the question, my mother said.

JPW I should think so.

Irish Man No. But she said she was sorry they'd made such a long journey for nothing but 'twas their own fault and then she sent them packing.

JPW Good! Well now, when did the old voice break so that we can start motoring?

Irish Man But they weren't to be put off that easy.

JPW They came back?

Irish Man They came back, pleading. They said I'd have a share of the profits. Well-a, my father said – he was still alive at the time. After all, he said, there's no great harm in it.

Not that my mother ever paid much heed to him. She always looked to Abramo, me eldest brother. Abramo was the real figure of authority in our house.

JPW What did Abramo say?

Irish Man Well, my mother got a little surprise because, after thinking, Abramo said that he personally couldn't see anything in it to frown about. (*A smile of minor triumph.*) Hah?

JPW Very interesting, truly, Benimillo, but I think I have now got sufficient data on that area.

Irish Man No –

JPW So many other areas to audit.

Irish Man No –

JPW For instance, I played Yum-Yum, 'The Mikado' you know? at boarding school and came out of the experience comparatively unscathed.

Irish Man The next few weeks were fraught, fraught with excitement. Trips to Macerata, rehearsals, and we played, not in a grimy little hall, but in the municipal theatre. Someone had to push me on the stage. Then, suddenly, everything was all right and I sauntered back and forth with me parasol singing 'Passigiando un anno fa'. I couldn't hardly believe my ears that all the cries of 'Bis! Bis!' was really for me.

JPW Bis.

Irish Man To tell the God's honest truth, I felt ashamed like, getting so much more of the clapping than the others.

JPW *Your accent* – you must have been very young when you came to this country.

Irish Man But I'd filled the hall with my voice, held the crowd. They understood. And, I thought, I can do it again. I will do it again.

JPW But it was on to the building trade.

Irish Man I suppose the experience made me – giddy. But I don't know. 'Twas more than that. And 'twasn't the clapping. Like, you can talk forever, but singing. Singing, d'yeh know? The only possible way to tell people.

JPW What?

Irish Man (*shrugs, he does not know*) . . . Who are you? . . . But Abramo said, you may have been to . . . to . . . to –

JPW Macerata?

Irish Man Macerata, singing and play-acting, but that doesn't mean you forget your manners or the straits this family is in, and the job I had to look after.

JPW In the building trade?

Irish Man (*ire rising*) In the – what? – No! – The shop – messenger-boy – the local pharmacia, whatever the (*'Fuck that is.'*) – A shop-boy, messenger-boy, dogsbody – my brother was a tyrant!

JPW Good! Well, let us see now –

Irish Man (*harsh, intense, impotent hatred*) And the man I worked for, *he* was an alcoholic, a quack, a parasite, a failure in everything, ate rat poison one night and I came to this country shortly after!

JPW . . . I mean, that it is time, and I wanted to sum up.

Irish Man Sum up *what*?

JPW Your depression – that you are undergoing severe –

Irish Man What does that mean, depression?

JPW You can look it up for yourself.

Irish Man Everything mean and low?!

JPW Dispirited, humbled, yes, brought low.

Irish Man Everything mean and low?!

JPW Reduction in pitch of voice?

Irish Man Do you mean I'm unhappy?

JPW I should imagine so.

Irish Man Then I'm unhappy!

JPW That's good: anger, let it all come out. That is what I shall be aiming at.

Irish Man What have you been writing there?

JPW Confidential.

Irish Man What have you been writing down?

JPW Your file. Unethical –

Irish Man *snaps the sheet of paper from* **JPW**.

A matter between your GP and myself.

Irish Man (*reading*) 'Facts. There are too many facts in the world.'

JPW Interesting observation of yours.

Irish Man 'Fiction. Fantasy' (*He looks at* **JPW** *who averts his eyes.*) . . . 'Bis'.

JPW Encore?

Irish Man 'Towards the end of the session he smiled.'

JPW You did, we made progress.

Irish Man 'Pot of jam, tea, saccharin.'

JPW I do not take sugar. You might not think it, but I am still vain.

Irish Man Do you think I'm a fool?

JPW No. And I am not one either.

Irish Man You were summing up.

JPW That you are deeply unhappy – presently –

Irish Man Aren't you?

JPW And psychotic.

Irish Man Me?

JPW Yes.

Irish Man What's psychotic?

JPW Out of control.

Irish Man Is that so? (*Face contorted in impotent hatred.*) Anything else?

JPW You do not like what you are.

Irish Man Better than not knowing *who* or what I am!

JPW Another appointment in town, actually running late, but let me see, yes, I can manage, fortunately, another session tomorrow, same time – well, perhaps a little later. Twelve o'clock?

Irish Man I don't think so. (*Going out.*)

JPW I can make you sing! And remember –

Irish Man *is gone.*

. . . all drink out. (*He polishes off the remainder of his vodka.*) He's crazy.

He sticks a book in his pocket, is collecting up the money. **Mona** *is entering with some fruit and cigarettes for him.*

Mona Well, lover! Who was that I met on the stairs? (*She opens out the couch.*) How about a session?

He is already gone out the door. She puts down the fruit and the cigarettes.

No joy here, productive or otherwise! Here, there, elsewhere, where? Perhaps tonight. (*She crouches down as if talking to a child.*) So, little one, shall we go look at the sea? Too boring, cold, polluted? Bewley's then, again: tea and cakes. Or, the ezzo? (*Zoo.*) cinema? to see more shite. Ahm, we'll ah, we'll ah . . . be talking about it on the way home. Aa, fuck it, child, let's go somewhere.

She is leaving. Lights fading, up sound: Gigli singing 'O Paradiso'.

Scene Two

Off, church clock chiming twelve. **JPW** *huddled in bed in a drunken stupor, asleep. Bell on outer door ringing, silhouette of* **Irish Man** *coming to office door, knocking . . .*

Irish Man Mr King! . . . Mr King! . . .

Silhouette pacing to and fro for a few moments, then leaving. Lights fading, up sound: Gigli continuing 'O Paradiso'.

Scene Three

JPW *on phone.*

JPW Same answer I suppose. (*He nods gravely to her reply. Then:*) 'Bye . . . What? . . . Oh, couple of interviews in town and . . . Oh, what am I doing now, at this very moment? Stack of letters in front of me requiring attention and, you know, very busy . . . No, I'm still here . . . What? . . . I try . . . I promise . . . 'Bye. (*He puts the phone down.*) 'Please, please, don't phone me again.' I try. Helen.

He goes to the window and lets up the blind. Then reacting to someone watching his window from the street and into action: phone apparatus readjusted, bed reconverted, spectacles for effect, etc. He unlocks the door, opens it, sits on the couch confidently with a book, as if reading it. Church chiming two. **Irish Man** *has arrived. He stands in the doorway abjectly.*

This is a fine time of day! Come in!

Irish Man *continues, abject, in the doorway.*

But when I say twelve o'clock I mean twelve o'clock! Come in! (*He looks at* **Irish Man** *for the first time and becomes unnerved; he has to move.*) Well, to sing like Gigli in six easy lessons! . . . And how was your evening? Jolly? On the town? A trout from your stream? . . . Yes, well, but, I have to – shave. A beard is all very fine but bloody irritating stuff at this stage. (*He is moving towards the washroom.*)

Irish Man (*he doesn't look up*) Are you married?

JPW (*looks at him for a moment*) . . . Am I? Married?

Irish Man A saint is she.

JPW A saint is she yes, I must admit she is pretty special. Irish colleen, apron, you know? Darns my socks, that kind of thing.

Irish Man Children.

JPW Two. (*And retreating to the washroom.*) I am very fond of her and she is very fond of chintz.

Irish Man (*alone quietly*) I built a fire at home last night and burned all the toys in the house.

JPW (*off*) What?

Irish Man (*comes into the room*) What am I to do?

JPW (*off*) What?

JPW *now watching* **Irish Man** *from washroom doorway.*

Irish Man Everything so stale, so mean and low. Stupid, numbed, guilty, worthless, finished. . . . Finished? Naaw!

JPW You may smoke if you wish. (*Returns to the room.*)

Irish Man Do you live here, Mr King?

JPW No.

Irish Man I envy it.

JPW I don't.

Irish Man Then where do you live?

JPW Nothing very large, of course, but clematis round the door, that sort of dwelling. Perhaps in one of your own sylvan developments?

Irish Man With the wife?

JPW She does not have to darn my socks, of course, but that is her nature. Even when they have got no holes in them? (*He laughs. Silence. He sits.*) There's nothing staler than death, my friend.

Irish Man (*suddenly wild*) And what about me?!

JPW *uncomprehending.*

I! Me! I! What *I* want!

JPW And that is why we are here.

Irish Man What *I* feel!

JPW Check.

Irish Man Inside!

JPW Yes! Gigli.

Irish Man He's the devil!

JPW He's the? . . . Oh for God's sake, Benimillo, snap out of it.

Irish Man That's a – a stupid – ridiculous thing to say! D'yeh think I'd be this way if I could help it? When I listen to him – I-can't-stop-listening-to-him! Fills me! The – things – inside. Tense, everything more intense. And I listen carefully. And it's beautiful – But it's screaming! And it's longing. Longing for what? I don't know whether it's keeping me sane or driving me crazy. You may laugh.

JPW I am not laughing.

Irish Man Or is it mocking me?

JPW Music hath charms to –

Irish Man Naaw, whoever said that is a fool. And it has affected everything 'round me. A record! A Christmas present! I need to listen to him now!

JPW Disconnect him.

Irish Man I achieved things, boy. I come from nothing. Or what does it want me to do? Fly!

JPW Stop listening to him.

Irish Man I'll see it through. My wife is near nervous breakdown. She's barely holding on. She says I look like an old man. Hah?

JPW And so you do.

Irish Man She looks like an old woman. She was a princess. You should have seen her. Even three months ago. She's holding on for me she says, not the child. The child too, but why on earth for me? And I burned all his toys last night. I rooted them out of every corner. And I'm so proud of him. I see him watching me sometimes. He's almost nine. I watch him sometimes too, secretly, and wonder will I write him a letter. Or take him for a little walk, my arm around his shoulders. Because, though he's nearly nine, and a boy, he would still allow me put my arm around his shoulders. My son. And explain to him that I don't matter. That it would be better if I disappeared.

JPW Ah, Mr –

Irish Man And sometimes I wish them things (*'Dead.'*) that I don't want to wish them, things that are maybe going to turn out unlucky.

JPW Ah, Mr –

Irish Man My wife come down last night. Nightdress, long hair. I pretended I didn't hear her come in or that she was watching me. And I kept listening to the music. Then she come and stood beside my chair. Smiling. And she said, what are you listening to. I use the headphones at night. Elgar, I said. I don't know why I said that because the only thing I listen to is him. And. You off I said. To bed. And she said yes, it's ten past one heighho. And. You coming up she said. And I said, in a little, I said. And. Then she knelt down and put her head on my knees. And then she said talk to me. Talk to me, talk to me, please love talk to me. And I couldn't think of a single thing to say. And then she said, I love you so much. And I said I love you too . . . but not out loud. And. Then she got up. And then she said pull yourself together, what's the matter with you, for God's sake get a grip on yourself, pull yourself together. She was trembling. She'd let go for a moment. And then she said goodnight. When she left I stood up. Out of respect. I knew she would've stopped in the hall. She usually does. Just stands there for a few moments. Before going up. And. Then it came out. My roar. Fuck you, fuck you . . . fuck you. (*Though delivered quietly and the intense emotion contained, tears have started down the* **Irish Man**'s *face during the speech.*)

JPW Ah, Mr . . . I'm out of my depth . . . This organisation, Steve, our founder, leader, came over and set up this office. Though I have always wanted to achieve something, I couldn't do even that much on my own. They sent me over here. But even they have forgotten me. And I have forgotten them. I

think it is likely they shipped Steve back to the States. I do
not even know if we are still in existence.

Irish Man Then-why-do-you-stay-on-in-this-terrible-country-
then!

JPW (*a gesture to the window, 'Helen', changes his mind, and follows
with the peculiarly defensive reply under the circumstances*) That's –
that is my affair! I'm out of my depth.

Irish Man	No, you're not –
JPW	I'm out of my depth!
Irish Man	No, you're not.
JPW	I have no answers, I'm at my wit's end –
Irish Man	No, you're not, no you're not –
JPW	Good grief, trying to work things out, all my life, for myself.

Irish Man Your Helen, your dwelling, your –

JPW Yes, my – That is none of your business!

Irish Man I'm happy with you.

JPW There is no organisation! –

Irish Man I'm happy with you, Mr King –

JPW A real, recognised, qualified, university-trained psychiatrist you need.

Irish Man *rolling his head.*

What have you against them?

Irish Man They don't know! Philosophy! And people like
them – I've dealt with them – I've had them on the building
sites – walking fast in pinstripe suits – that's all they know –
or fucked-up by too much education – that's all they know!

JPW They can see patterns.

Irish Man I'm happy with you.

JPW	(*'No.'*) I don't mind making a fast buck –
Irish Man	I have a lot of time for instinct –
JPW	I don't mind telling you I need the shillings –
Irish Man	Always used instinct –
JPW	But, in fairness, I drew the line. I am not, though you might think it, a ponce.

Irish Man Instinct, my strength, boy. Unerring instinct for the right man for the job.

JPW This is not a job!

Irish Man I'll get to the root of this, I'll see it through, my way. I've never been beaten – Oh, they tried, but I left a few cripples around the place. I've taken on, done business with the big – (*Whispers.*) the biggest in the land – and there was nothing he, or they, could teach little me. Never been beaten, a survivor, and this isn't going to beat me either.

JPW Gently for a second. For what it is worth, my opinion: in any game it is dangerous taking up arms against an unknown enemy.

Irish Man (*hand in pocket*) And if all comes to all, I have the trump card.

JPW Gently, for a second. Are we talking about singing? I mean, can you be serious?

Irish Man Oh, I'm always serious –

JPW To sing! –

Irish Man I could never afford to be anything but serious!

JPW Benimillo –

Irish Man I'm so serious –

JPW Benimillo! –

Irish Man You look out – you-look-out! – cause I'm going to get you too!

JPW (*silently*) Well-well.

Irish Man So is my time up for today?

JPW I should imagine it is. I have some meditating to do.

Irish Man So what time tomorrow?

JPW Tomorrow is Saturday, I do not work weekends.

Irish Man I'll pay you in advance? – For the remaining four sessions. Cash or – it'll have to be a cheque.

JPW And you want a session on Sunday? Well-well. That was not a very kind thing to say to a friend, Benimillo.

Irish Man How much?

JPW Double-time for Saturday and Sunday.

Irish Man How much?

JPW A round figure?

Irish Man A hundred pounds.

JPW Gosh! (*'A hundred pounds.'*) Your desperation is fantastic.

Irish Man Always conscious of money but I was never interested in it.

JPW A hundred is fine and a cheque is fine and the banks are still open.

Irish Man What time tomorrow?

JPW Your choice.

Irish Man You'll be here?

JPW State the time.

Irish Man You'll be here?

JPW I'll be here.

Irish Man (*about to hand over the cheque, remembers*) I'll be back with cash in two minutes.

Irish Man *goes out.*

JPW Nearly got your second name, *Benimillo!* . . . Jesus Christ!

JPW *reflective, then a short kicking dance, two feet off the ground at the same time, reflective again, an idea; he uncovers a classified telephone directory, finds a number, adjustment to telephone apparatus . . .*

Hospitals, hospitals. What am I doing? – He's crazy! St Anne's, administration, nurses' residence, X-ray department. No. St Godolph's unusual one, administration, nurses' – ah! (*Raps out a number.*) Psychiatric department, please . . . Good afternoon. The psychiatrist in charge, please . . . his assistant then . . . any psychiatrist . . . yes, an appointment . . . no, for my brother . . . for today . . . next month! . . . Couldn't she see me tomorrow? . . . I know tomorrow is Saturday, Miss, but I have got my brother outside, now, literally tied up with ropes in the boot of the car . . . Miss, I'm a practising GP and this is not a case for your casualty department . . . Madam, I am sitting on a barrel of gun powder, can-you-help-me? . . . Monday. What time? . . . That's very early . . . I said that is fine . . . What? . . . Oh, Mickeleen O'Loughlin. (*He puts phone down.*)

Irish Man *returns and slaps the money on the desk.*

Irish Man Noon tomorrow! And you had better be here! Do you understand that?

JPW *striking pose head to head with* **Irish Man** *across the desk.*

JPW Bring your pistols! I'll bring the booze!

Up music, final section of 'O Paradiso', to conclude the scene.

Scene Four

JPW *and* **Mona** *in bed, swapping a bottle of vodka.* **JPW** *drinking hard to fortify himself. On the floor beside the bed some new books, charts; some groceries on the desk.*

Mona *is thirty-eight. Her moods can alternate as quickly as her thoughts, but her vitality, generosity and seemingly celebratory nature allow her to hold a 'down' mood only fleetingly. She is dressed in a white slip.*

Mona You're not listening to me.

He nods.

I shouldn't have dropped in?

He nods.

You're bored now?

He nods. She kicks him or whatever.

And-I-was-ravenous. So I dashed out and took my god-child to her ballet class. Dashed back home. Pacing the floor: what to do now? *And-I-was-still-ravenous* – for something. So I ate three eggs, then two yoghurts: still wondering, what'll I have now? So I thought I'll chance you.

JPW Well, I am going to see this thing through too.

Mona You're not listening to me!

JPW I am. He may even shoot me if I don't.

Mona Who?

JPW Benimillo. A practical man, like my father. But this practical man is declaring that the romantic kingdom *is* of this world.

Mona And that's all you were doing last night, reading?

JPW I *want* him to prove it. I am contracted to assist him.

Mona If I had known.

JPW Do you see what I mean? And I have been up all night.

Mona I could have come over – to assist you.

JPW And I had it all figured out at one point. They said I'd never achieve anything. I got very excited.

She is lying on top of him or snuggling up to him.

Pardon? No! You should not be doing this to me.

Mona Seducing you, lover?

JPW Yes.

Mona It's freezing in here.

JPW It was all crystal clear.

Mona (*under the bedclothes*) Nothing much happening down here, my friend.

JPW No! No! You should not! And bringing those – groceries! – over here.

Mona You never talk about my problems any more.

JPW Now I have forgotten it all.

Mona Nobody does.

JPW What on earth am I to do?

Mona (*sighs to herself*) Keep on dreaming.

JPW I must keep it on a conversational level at all costs. But how does one do that?

Mona You keep on talking.

JPW Pardon?

Mona You keep on talking.

JPW Yes! Because, I mean to say, I am not *that* afraid of him.

Mona And shock them if you can.

JPW Yes, I'm sure he's a Catholic.

She laughs.

Are you a Catholic?

Mona (*nods*) And I pray.

JPW What is original sin?

Mona Fuck original sin.

JPW Existential guilt.

Mona What about my problems?!

JPW What problems?

Mona I'm a subject.

JPW You jump into bed as soon as you come in that door.

Mona That's my problem.

JPW I was lucky to escape the other day.

Mona That's why I came early this morning. (*She gets up, starts to dress.*)

JPW What are you doing?

Mona Another port of call.

JPW Where to?

Mona Oh? A man. Does funny things to me. Are you jealous? You: fat chance.

JPW Don't go yet.

Mona All right. My chin is all sore, is it all red? What'll my husband say? I'm annoyed now I didn't think of batteries for your shaver.

JPW (*absently*) Did you think of a pot of jam?

Mona (*solemn nod 'Yes' and followed by a solemn tone as she gets back into bed*) But I have to collect my god-child. Then to the doctor.

JPW What-is-life?

Mona Life, my friend, is bouncing back. But, I suppose I was lucky to get in here at all, hmm? The bars are going up around town against old Mona. And some – curtain – is being drawn. Jimmy. Promise me something. That you'll let me down gently.

JPW What are you talking about?

Mona Now that you ask. I'm not quite sure. Or where I am or what I'm at. I know there's someone else – I've always known it – but I'm not too bad, am I?

JPW (*defensively*) What someone else?

Mona But I know it. But I *know* it! Look at you now: eyes like a wounded – nun.

JPW I'm forty-six.

Mona Great man for your age all right. Who is she? – I mean just for interest's sake.

JPW I'm very flattered.

Mona I'm twenty-eight. Thirty-eight. And nothing to show for it yet. When I get into bed with you I say right Mona, down to work, fifteen times today.

JPW We did it twice the time before last.

Mona *My* doing. And you're only a baby – all men are babies – and I'd hate to have big tits.

JPW I never said –

Mona Some men do! (*Then she laughs.*) In the past. Promise. Like a month's notice.

JPW 'In the past'. And all your 'dashing' around town at night? 'But I *know* it'.

Mona I always try here first.

JPW Well, you shouldn't.

Mona Well, what is it about me, tell me? – as against Miss-whoever-she-is. And she doesn't look after you very well, does she? (*She indicates the room.*)

JPW You are a respectable married woman!

Then they laugh. Then she becomes grave.

Mona Don't laugh at me. You don't know what it's like.

JPW What?

Mona (*mutters*) 'Good old Mona.' *And*, I don't like being used.

JPW Yes, well, but, Mona, I sometimes feel –

Mona That's the first time you used my name today.

JPW Yes, but, well, I sometimes feel that you are possibly, I mean to say, using me. (*She nods gravely.*) I mean, the interesting thing, who picked up whom that evening in the supermarket?

Mona At the health-food counter.

JPW I have often wondered.

Mona My magician. And you are so gentle. I'll give you the money to have that phone reconnected.

JPW I'm a wage-earner now, I have a job.

Mona Suit yourself. Only, sometimes, I wish I could talk to you, hear that posh voice of yours.

JPW I have not got a posh voice.

Mona 'I have not got a – '

JPW Mona!

Mona All right, you have got a real west of Ireland accent.

JPW . . . What's wrong with this famous god-child of yours, Karen?

Mona (*insists*) Karen-Marie. (*Maree.*)

JPW Karen-Marie.

Mona I'm going to the doctor.

JPW What's wrong with you?

Mona I fancy the doctor.

JPW I wouldn't put it past you.

Mona Where would you put it? . . . You don't like those remarks.

He gets it and laughs.

But, at least you deign to talk to me when I'm here. Not like some. And not like that string of misery I have at home. (*She grunts in imitation of her husband.*) I'm leaving him. Don't worry, not because of you. And I have him worn out too. (*Sighs.*) I should have married a farmer.

JPW Six children.

Mona Double it. Now you're getting close. Here, I'll give you a laugh. You know how I take that god-child everywhere with me? But-can-I-stop-her-dawdling-behind! We were shopping during the week and we had to go through the men's wear department to get to the ladies' wear and suddenly this voice, 'Madam! Madam!' This poor shop-assistant, eighty, if he was a day. And I looked around for Karen-Marie. And you know shop-dummies? Well, there she was, innocent as you like, looking up at their faces, unzipping their flies and putting her hand inside. 'Madam! Madam!' And I'm shouting . . . There's someone outside.

Silhouette of **Irish Man** *arriving outside, tapping the door.*

Is that him?

JPW Stay where you are.

Mona Ah, Jimmy –

JPW I shan't be long, Benimillo! (*Silhouette moving away.*) No, let him wait – bloody hell – he's early. What am I going to say to him? Unzipping their flies, putting her hand inside, putting her hand inside.

Mona (*continues in a whisper, dressing hurriedly*) 'Madam!
Madam!' And I'm shouting 'Karen-Marie! Karen-Marie!'
'Madam! Madam!' 'Karen-Marie! Karen-Marie!' And says
Karen-Marie – (*To* **JPW**.) Don't be looking at me
(*Dressing.*) – 'They're only dummies', she said, 'they have
no willies'. Well laugh!

JPW They have no willies. (*Putting on his trousers, etc.*)

Mona And the other women about were in hysterics.

JPW And what happened then?

Mona And what happened then . . . (*She appears peculiarly
lost for a moment.*) I think I'm going crazy. Am I forgetting
anything?

Off, church clock chiming twelve.

Jesus! – Twelve o'clock! – How do I get out of here?

JPW He's not my wife.

Mona You haven't got a wife. (*Adjusting her bodice, referring to
her breasts.*) If it fits in your mouth it's big enough. See yeh,
get the phone mended will yeh, see yeh.

*He lets her out and shuts the door. He is smoking, drinking, leaves the
bed unconverted – trying to assert a defiance – opens the door on the last
chime of the church clock, strikes a pose with a chart or book, his back
to the door, and waits.*

Irish Man *comes to stand in the doorway, smiling; he is carrying a
large cardboard box. He looks pleased with himself this morning.*

Irish Man Can I come in?

JPW (*curt*) Come in.

Irish Man I arrived a bit early I'm afraid. Can I come in?

JPW Come in.

Irish Man I did a little shopping. Can I come in?

JPW It must be spoken three times. Come in!

Irish Man I couldn't ring the bell because of these. I brought the pistols. Can I put it here? . . . Hah? . . . Hah? . . . It's easy enough put together . . . Hah?

Irish Man *chuckling 'Hah', producing a new record-player from the box, and a record.*

JPW *is thrown, surprised and resentful of this move, but trying to contain himself.*

JPW You mean to say you bought that?

Irish Man Hah? The wife? (*Mona.*)

JPW No, not the wife, Benimillo. Drink? While I am *waiting* for you.

Irish Man Hah? Thanks, yes, why not, please.

JPW Oh?

Irish Man Weekend. She was wearing a ring.

JPW She wasn't! Begod! Another man's wife, Benimillo, are you shocked?

Irish Man Good luck!

JPW She's a Catholic.

Irish Man And what does your own wife think about all this in your sylvan dwelling?

JPW *reacts angrily, sweeping the groceries off the desk into drawers of wherever.*

. . . I didn't mean to offend you or . . . Wha'?

JPW Ah, sure man dear alive, a mac, sure I know well you didn't sure! And that machine set you back a few quid, five or six hundred?

Irish Man Are you having an affair, Mr King?

JPW She may think so.

Irish Man Oh now, that's a bit chauvinist.

JPW (*'Gosh! Chauvinist!'*) What did you think of her?

Irish Man A fine woman.

JPW But her tits – you don't fancy big tits then?

Irish Man Is there a power-point somewhere?

JPW I knew this Irish chap once had a big thing about (*Mimes.*) round electric light switches.

Irish Man (*finds the power-point*) Here we are.

JPW Ah but sure if it fits in your mouth it's big enough.

Irish Man Anything more is a waste. (*In reaction to* **JPW***'s surprise.*) That's what we used to say all right. If it fits in your mouth it's big enough, anything more is a waste.

JPW But, but – personally, Benimillo – big or small, they are startling things, and I am always astonished at how casually the ladies themselves take them for granted.

Irish Man There we are. (*Set up.*)

JPW Would you agree with that observation?

Irish Man (*switches on machine – orchestral opening bars of 'O Paradiso'*) D'yeh mind?

JPW I do.

Irish Man (*cueing to another track*) No, not this first one, it starts with 'O Paradiso' but there's a piece here –

JPW I said I do mind!

Irish Man Wha'?

JPW I said no, Benimillo, no! (*He switches off the machine.*)

Irish Man I just want you to listen to him.

JPW I said no! You want to listen to him or you want to sing like him, which? Sit down. We have work to do. Look at this chart, please. (*He holds up a chart or he draws a chart – three circles, connecting lines, etc. – on the wall.*)

Irish Man (*placatory*) I enjoy our meetings, Mr King.

JPW You see this circle here, the most perfect of shapes, the cosmic womb, the perfect state, the clear pool of being. We travel down this line –

Irish Man I look forward to them.

JPW We travel down this line to our second pool, existence, the here and now. Again the most perfect of shapes, but look at what is inside: a mess.

Irish Man I enjoy them.

JPW Circles within circles, concentric and eccentric, squiggles, swirls of objects, and at the bottom, this dark area here, sediment, despair. Our problem, to achieve the state of clear which exists here, in our second pool, here. But, paradoxically, it is from this dark area, this rising darkness of our despair that the solution is to derive, if – if! – we can get it to rise to cover the whole pool and blot out our squiggles and circles and what-nots. Good.

Irish Man What's the third pool?

JPW Indeed. And I should be grateful if you did not interrupt me further. The areas we shall be going into from here on in are not without risk, and will demand not only your concentration, but that courage required for an encounter of a most strange and singular kind.

Irish Man You're having me on. (*Smiling, uneasy with this kind of talk.*)

JPW Pardon?

Irish Man Aw!

JPW 'Aw'?

Irish Man Naaw!

JPW 'Naaw'? You are not saying, I hope, that you thought the simple problem you have set us would be solved in the traditional way? I mean by sitting down together and playing that game called Slobs. The winner proves himself to be the most sentimental player and becomes King Slob by dealing, at the most unexpected moment, a sudden judas punch, or an emotional kick in the genitals to his opponent, thereby *getting* him. Problem solved.

Irish Man I was out of sorts yesterday.

JPW But we had a good night last night, had we, slept well?

Irish Man No.

JPW The three aspects which we shall concentrate on today are, one, your existential guilt, two, its twin paralysing demon, the I-am-who-am syndrome, and three, despair. Then, if you are up to it, we shall over the next three days set to possibilising that quiet power of the possible waiting within you.

Irish Man Naaw, aw!

JPW 'Naaw – aw' again! Explain yourself. Ah! You are impatient to ask what is your natural existential guilt.

Irish Man Guilt – exist – I'm not guilty of anything.

JPW	Heard you yesterday, imprisoned, numbed, guilty.
Irish Man	Survival! – What am I guilty of, survival? D'yeh know what's going on out there?
JPW	The point is you feel guilty.
Irish Man	And innocent at the same time!

JPW That's good. Just like Adam when he got the boot.

Irish Man (*silently*) *Adam!*

JPW What have I done he said to God, I only – But God said, out, out!

Irish Man You're having me on!

JPW But what had Adam done? No, it was not a deed. Adam did not lose his head over Eve in the Garden, he lost his tail – when he bit the apple. He *gained* a head, knowledge – Tree of Knowledge – a little of which, one bite, is a dangerous thing. He started thinking – *thinking* – and self-consciousness crept in, which is existential guilt, which is original sin.

Irish Man I don't know what you're talking about!

JPW Indeed, I contend, that it was much later that the screwing started. Mind-numbing screwing to stop those very feelings of simultaneous innocence and guilt and, naturally, finding themselves out in the cold, simply to keep themselves warm, the creatures.

Irish Man What's this got to do with it?

JPW On to clearing the jungle, developing it, mind-numbing drudgery to stop the pain of what they had lost. On to milking the goats, cutting the grass, trying to get Cain to toe a more conservative and respectable line, standardised activity, routine trivia, looking for the new security.

Irish Man *You* don't know what you're talking about!

JPW (*confronting* **Irish Man**) And all the time further obliterating that side of their nature that was innocent and beautiful, as if it were the side that is vulgar, vicious, mean, ruthless, offensive, dangerous, obscene. Benimello, what are you doing? Benimillo!

Irish Man *has gone to record-player and cued in a track. He faces* **JPW** *squarely, a dangerous and warning attitude telling* **JPW** *not to interfere. Gigli singing 'Dai campi, dai prati'. They listen to the complete aria including the final orchestral bars.* **Irish Man**'s *attitude softens through the aria and, perhaps, a few whimper-like sounds escape.* **JPW** *conceals his appreciation of the singing. At the conclusion* **Irish Man** *switches off the machine and waits with a childlike expectation for an appreciative reaction.*

Irish Man Wha'? . . . Hah? . . . That's not my favourite, but because of that I thought you might like it best . . . Wha'?

JPW Did you have your tonsils out?

Irish Man What? . . . I didn't! What did you think of him?

JPW Sobs a bit much, doesn't he, pouts a bit much?

Irish Man That's the snobbery I was talking about!

JPW And those 'h' sounds.

Irish Man King!

JPW (*has picked up the record sleeve*) Yes, 'Beniamino'.

Irish Man (*muttering furiously*) Oh but the English, the English, what would they know anyway.

JPW Do you know what he is singing?

Irish Man You don't have to! –

JPW Do you understand the words? –

Irish Man You don't –

JPW What opera was that piece from? –

Irish Man You don't have to know! I could always size a man up more from the sound he makes than from what he's saying.

JPW Your unerring instinct. (*Looking at record sleeve.*) 'Mefistofele': ah yes, he *is* the devil.

Irish Man We were making little gold crosses over here when ye, over there, were still living in holes in the ground.

JPW I do not doubt your word on it but what precisely is your point?

Irish Man I hate yeh!

JPW Sorry about that, old boy, but would we now choose to be superior if we could help it?

Irish Man Oh, but very cold people the English, the British – Oh! and your Empire: that's located somewhere now in – what's them little islands called?

JPW Oh, come, you can do better than that, you who have dealt and fenced and parried with the highest in the land. Have another drink, it will stimulate you. Here.

Irish Man *sends a chair careering across the room with a kick: he is about to smash his glass, and possibly* **JPW** *as well.*

Irish Man Do you know who you're dealing with?

JPW Be my guest (*Smash the glass.*) . . . I find I am not afraid of you. Despite the path you have left behind you strewn with cripples – and corpses? Jail, hospital, or – (*Mimes shooting himself in the head.*) mean nothing to me either. But I have only two glasses remaining in the house and if you smash that one, I shall certainly break this precious bottle over your head before you make a second move.

Irish Man (*a warning*) Don't try to take him (*Gigli.*) away from me, Mr King.

JPW On the contrary. I am beginning to find this project most exciting. I intend to see it through. You say similarly, but I have an instinct too, and something is bothering me about *your* commitment. (*He pours drinks.*)

Irish Man To sing!

JPW That's good! Repeat it.

Irish Man To sing, to sing!

JPW And I want you to go on repeating it. Yes, cheers! Because the most dangerous approach to our work from here-on-in is the half-longing half-frightened one. Look at our chart, please – the third pool, the one you asked about. One false step and not only do you miss your target but you end up out here, pool three, questionmark pool, banana-land!

Irish Man (*helping himself to another drink*) You'd know about it out there!

JPW I am simply obliged to warn you.

Irish Man Cheers-cheers-cheers!

JPW And you may never come back.

Irish Man What of it?

JPW Indeed! (*Laughing, getting carried away with himself.*) You may never come back to the poxy, boring anchor of this everyday world you have sold your soul for!

Irish Man What of it?

JPW The poxy boring anchor of this everyday world that others of us are shut out from!

Irish Man What of it!

JPW Indeed! The choice is yours! But I must be convinced of your commitment, and –

Irish Man Wait a minute –

JPW You are the one, to my mind, beginning to falter.

Irish Man Wait a minute, what did you say?

JPW What did I say?

Irish Man There's something all along not making sense.

JPW Well, of course, I have not as yet explained the paralysing I-am-who-am syndrome.

Irish Man No. The poxy everyday world that others of us are shut out from?

JPW Pardon?

Irish Man This house of yours, sylvan dwelling – this wife of yours?

JPW Allow me to complete my thesis, please.

Irish Man No. Them groceries, two glasses in the house – this wife of yours?

JPW Questions, if you have any, on the foregoing, please –

Irish Man You have a very strange life of it here, Mr King –

JPW Otherwise, please allow me to continue.

Irish Man Are you separated, Mr King?

JPW Questions on the subject to hand, please –

Irish Man Divorced?

JPW Well, there goes our session.

Irish Man There's something wrong somewhere.

JPW Thank you, that will be all for today. (*He has opened the door.*)

Irish Man No.

JPW Yes, I am conducting things here.

Irish Man (*smiling, assessing*) Hah? (*Then he laughs.*)

JPW (*bluffing*) Or – and I am loath to suggest it –
because you have indicated a dissatisfaction with my mode
of procedure, you would rather perhaps we discontinued the
whole thing entirely?

Irish Man No –

JPW Yes! – and had a refund of your money? . . . Yes?

Irish Man (*considers, then calls* **JPW***'s bluff*) Yes.

JPW I mean to say.

Irish Man I suppose it'll have to be a refund. You owe me
sixty-five pounds.

JPW . . . Well, a refund is not going to be entirely possible.

Irish Man You owe me sixty-five quid.

JPW I owe you –

Irish Man Three sessions –

JPW No, I don't!

Irish Man The first ten, the second –

JPW The first session, fifteen! Since you are not completing
the course.

Irish Man Okay. The first fifteen, the second ten, third
ten –

JPW Twenty!

Irish Man That's thirty-five pounds.

JPW Twenty, Saturday, double-time!

Irish Man Which leaves sixty-five outstanding.

JPW Hold, sir, please! Third, today, twenty.

Irish Man You're charging me double for today?

JPW Look at the time! Forty-five pounds. You gave me a hundred, which leaves fifty-five, not sixty-five.

Irish Man Okay. We agreed –

JPW A round figure.

Irish Man Yes, the hundred that I gave you yesterday.

JPW Yes. Which leaves –

Irish Man On top of that I gave you fifteen on the first day, I gave you a total of a hundred and fifteen. Look, I'm not interested in the money.

JPW Nor I.

Irish Man Yes.

JPW No. (*'Nor I.'*)

Irish Man What?

JPW I agree.

Irish Man So do I.

JPW I think we should continue too.

Irish Man So do I. But.

JPW What?

Irish Man . . . But. Forty-five from a hundred and fifteen, you calculate it.

JPW That is correct.

Irish Man You owe me seventy pounds! Not sixty-five or fifty-five!

JPW (*offering money*) Your name will be included in the draw next week for the rest of it.

Irish Man (*refusing money*) Not interested in the money . . . So what do we do?

JPW Well, I don't know, *Benimillo*.

Irish Man Well. (*Going to the door. Bluffing about leaving.*) Do we continue tomorrow? It's up to you.

JPW You don't have to go right now. Do you? I mean to say, Saturday – I'm flexible. And we were approaching certain disturbing areas back there and, frankly, a crying shame to cut off when we are on the point of some possibly – nitty-gritty. Hmm?

Irish Man *nods solemnly.*

Have a little drink and we'll take five.

Irish Man Well, a little one.

JPW There. Good luck!

Irish Man Cheers!

JPW Start, stop, cue in, cue out, repeat buttons, nice machine. (*He catches* **Irish Man** *smiling in satisfaction to himself.*) You are a bit of a bastard, Benimillo.

Irish Man (*chuckling*) You're not so bad yourself.

They laugh; more drinks; eyes on the record-player; then laughing again and silent again, their eyes on the machine – the machine a reminder of what has to be achieved.

Irish Man Was there anything at all in that talk of yours?

JPW Frankly, I cannot remember a word of if.

Laughter. **JPW** *closes the door. They are getting quite drunk. Drinking through the following. Absently, they pull their chairs to the machine and sit there as if around a fire.*

Irish Man You're not married. Just as there's no house, sylvan dwelling, there's no wife.

JPW I am entitled to a little fantasy too.

Irish Man You're not married! – You're not married! – never were! – Now!

JPW Isn't your triumph in this discovery excessive?

Irish Man Now! I enjoy our sessions.

JPW So do I! . . . (*Quietly.*) But there is a woman.

Irish Man Yeh? . . . That brought yeh to your knees? . . . Not the lady, that nice woman that was here?

JPW (*silently*) No.

Irish Man Yeh?

JPW You want to talk about me?

Irish Man It's only fair.

JPW You are not writing a book, Benimillo? Gosh, you are laughing again!

Irish Man She's a beauty? – Wha'? – Helen – Yeh?

JPW Yes. Beauty: a shy, simple, comely, virtuous, sheltered, married maiden. The resolution to all my problems, whatever they are.

Irish Man Someone to darn your socks.

JPW Yes. That would be an achievement.

Irish Man Always the married ones?

JPW No. I'm unlucky. The discovery that she was already married deterred me but, after six months of it, I could not stop myself and I wrote to her my confession of love. Such a thing to her madonna face was out of the question.

His laughter, punctuating the story, is pitiful and it sounds more like crying.

Irish Man Yeh?

JPW She requested an interview which I granted in a car park. The sheltered married maiden's reply to my confession, 'Why do men always take me by surprise?' I was struck dumb: her husband apart, I was not the first to notice her beguiling innocence and domestic potential. When I recovered from the shock of this, I realised I was serious about her. And began a series of written and oral entreaties which were to continue for a number of years.

Irish Man How many?

JPW Four. All to no avail . . . The thing was getting out of hand . . . This simple married maiden was proving to be a peculiar combination of flirtatious and seductive behaviour which, having aroused me, instantly turned to resistance and rejection. She was now my sole goal in life, and I neglected all else. Would you believe, even a call to Mama's deathbed. I was otherwise engaged.

Irish Man Two children?

JPW (*nods*) I made a vow: I would celibate myself, keep myself pure for her. And I added the further precaution of becoming vegetarian, and eating only health foods. And further, I swore that if she should come to bed with me for one short hour and sweet, I would repay her by ending my life there and then.

Irish Man You told her that?

JPW Why not? A present of a locket was not going to be much use in this case . . . One short sweet hour to allow my wounds to bleed . . . And I would say to her in the car park, how remarkable, you and I alive in Time at the same time. And she would say, but why me? What fate is following me that wreaks havoc in men's hearts, they lose all care for themselves, their jobs, their everything.

Irish Man She was having a great time.

JPW She –

Irish Man Oh she was leading you a merry dance.

JPW No.

Irish Man Oh, I know Irishwomen.

JPW No.

Irish Man She was making a right fool of you.

JPW Benimillo! (*Indicating the door.*)

Irish Man And she still is.

JPW I will not have it! Not from you! You are a very bitter and twisted little man and I'll thank you to keep your opinions to yourself.

Irish Man Okay! Yeh?

JPW She was very upset.

Irish Man You said it brought you to your knees.

JPW Did I? Well, it is not finished yet. She phones me every single day!

Irish Man Yeh?

JPW After a number of final meetings she requested a final meeting. So we met. A hurried meeting: she had even forgotten to take her apron off which I glimpsed beneath her overcoat and which tugged strangely at my heart strings. She said you are a remarkable man and goodbye. Do not regret it, she said, but you must, you *must*, forget me.

Irish Man Regret what?

JPW You do not understand.

Irish Man Don't regret what, you done nothing.

JPW Benimillo! We were having an affair with the Gods! And despite the agony I felt a wonder . . . yes, wonder . . . that I should be capable of such sustained intensity about someone and about something for a change . . . Do not regret it, she said, but you must forget me, and though we can never meet again I shall feel energised at every recurrence of your memory. Happiness and beauty are not meant to mate.

Irish Man And that was it?

JPW Yeh. That evening I met, oh, someone in a supermarket and thus ended four years of celibacy.

Irish Man Aw, they're strange people, women. You can forget her.

JPW Well, we shall finish *our* little job first, then we shall see. (*He switches on the record-player. Gigli singing 'Toselli's Serenade'.*)

Irish Man (*'Wait'll you hear about my one.'*) Her name was Ida. (*His gestures, drunkenness, becoming operatic.*)

JPW (*turns down volume a little*) Hmm?

Irish Man Her name was Ida. She had a grand, a lovely speaking voice, d'yeh know, and I felt-a drawn to her without ever having clapped an eye on her.

JPW She was a radio announcer.

Irish Man Wha'? No! She was a telephonist. I'd never dare go near such a beauty, but, after all, it was on the phone, and I asked her would she like to go for a little walk. The simple way she said yes (*Gave him a great feeling.*). I'd never took a girl out before but I walked happy-as-larry, bliss, Mr

King, at her side. Looking at the fountains, the monuments, the – wha'?

JPW *has started muttering.*

JPW Milano? Macerata? Recanati?

Irish Man No! Later! Rome! The beggars begging, the English ladies reading poetry, and the lovely little peasant girls that worked as artists' models waiting to be choosed. Wha'?

JPW Dante? – the poetry – Nothing. You married Ida?

Irish Man No! I had to go 'way. But when I come back I rang the exchange. She didn't work there any more. 'She's been behaving very strange lately,' one of the other telephone girls told me.

JPW Indiscreet remark from a colleague.

Irish Man Wha'?

JPW Go on.

Irish Man I ran to her house.

JPW Dead!

Irish Man No! You-a go way-a (*'You go away.'*) her mother said. Please, I said, let me see her. Ida was in hospital.

JPW Close.

Irish Man She had a nervous breakdown. O-o-o!

JPW A sore thing.

Irish Man I ran to the hospital and put the little bunch of flowers on her bed and waited for her to laugh or to cry or to throw open her arms. But she only turned her head away. Her voice – it didn't sound like a voice at all: tired, faint, d'yeh know, distant. Don't you understand, she said, it's no use.

JPW Whatever could she mean?

Irish Man I fought them, she said. Them? Her mother and father. I held out for ages, she said, but they said it'd kill them. So I gave in. Then I started fainting all the time, she said, now I'm getting better, but I've promised them.

JPW 'Promised them what'? (*Mimicking* **Irish Man**.)

Irish Man Never to see you again.

JPW 'But why?'!

Irish Man 'But why?' Oh, nothing, she said. You're poor, she said, they say I might as well marry a beggar, they say you'll end up singing in the streets.

JPW Aha!

Irish Man But, Ida! Don't insist, she said, slow, she said, slow, I've changed, she said, it's no use, you see, I don't love you no more. I couldn't believe it! I rushed from that room, boy. I never saw Ida again.

His Ida story concludes with the conclusion of 'Toselli's Serenade'.

JPW What do you think of whore-houses, Benimillo? I could recommend a good one. People there dress up as bishops and things.

Irish Man But don't yeh see: the similarities between your story and mine?

JPW My story is about a real live living person, your story is bullshit. What are you laughing at? (*Beginning to laugh also.*) What are you laughing at?

Irish Man One short sweet hour with her, you said, and you'd give your life: I'd give my life for one short sweet hour to be able to sing like that.

JPW (*privately, not convinced*) Would you?

Irish Man (*going out unsteadily*) One short sweet hour (*Off.*) One short sweet hour.

JPW *alone.*

Evening light has set in during the above, now further deepening to night light. Gigli – muted – singing 'Cielo e mar' timed to conclude with end of the scene.

JPW You see, Benimillo, God created the world in order to create himself. Us. We are God. But that neatly done he started making those obscure and enigmatic statements. Indeed his son did a lot of rather the same thing. The Last Supper, for instance: the wine, the conversation, *Jewish* wine being passed around. (*He rises unsteadily.*) Christ standing up, 'In a little while you will see me, in a little while you will not see me.' They must have thought the man was drunk. But he had learned the lingo from his father. God taking his stroll in the Garden, as we were told, and passing by innocent Adam, he would nod, and say (*He nods and winks.*) 'I am who am.' And that was fine until one day, Adam, rather in the manner of Newton, was sitting under a tree and an apple fell on his head jolting him into thought. 'Whatever can he mean,' said Adam, ''I am who am''?' And he waited until the next time God came strolling by, and he said, 'Excuse me' – or whatever they said in those days. I must find out. And he put the question to God. But God said, 'Out, out!' 'I only asked!' said Adam. But God said, 'Out!' And, naturally, after such rude, abrupt and despotic eviction, the wind was taken out of Adam's intellectual sails: not surprising that he was not up to pursuing the matter. Which is a pity. Because, the startling thing, God had got it wrong. Because what does it mean, 'I am who am'? It means this is me and that's that. This is me and I am stuck with it. You see? Limiting. What God should have been saying, of course, was 'I am who may be'. Which is a different thing, which makes sense – both for us and for God – which means I am the possible, or, if you prefer, I am the impossible. Yes, it is all crystal clear.

Mona *arrives outside and remains, briefly, to knock and call his name. He ignores her and she goes away.*

Mona Jimmy? . . . Jimmy?

JPW Yes, yes, it is all crystal clear. We understand our existential guilt, our definition of ourselves is right from the start – I am who may be – and, meanwhile, our paradoxical key, despair, is rising, rising in our pool to total despair. That state achieved, two choices. One, okay, I give in, I wait for the next world. Or, two, what have I to lose, and I take the leap, the plunge into the abyss of darkness to achieve that state of primordial being, not in any muddled theocentric sense, but as the point of origin in the *here-and-now* where anything becomes possible. Now you follow! (*He laughs in celebration.*) And I have three more days to do it!

He turns up the volume: 'Cielo e mar', ending this scene triumphantly.

Scene Five

An intermission, if required, has taken place and the quartet from 'Rigoletto' introduces and continues into this scene.

JPW *dishevelled and exasperated;* **Irish Man** *also dishevelled – unusual for him – bewildered and carrying a hang-over.* **JPW** *has locked himself in the washroom:* **Irish Man** *is banging on the washroom door.*

Irish Man She's gone, gone, gone, left me!

JPW (*off*) I don't care, I don't care, I don't care!

Irish Man I called last night, you wouldn't let me in! I know you were in!

JPW (*off*) I was meditating!

Irish Man She took my son!

JPW *comes out angrily, clad in a blanket.*

JPW I don't care! Our fourth meeting, two to go and, frankly, you are confusing and boring the arse off me. (*Striding to the machine.*) Jesus, that machine! (*Switches it off.*) I went to bed last night with the repeat button switched on. I woke up this morning and it was still playing. Heaven knows what it has done to my brain! And speaking of singing, listen – (*Operating a button to the end of the quartet.*) Galli Curci, she is quite the best thing on it. (*He listens to the final notes. He switches off the record-player.*) Supernal last note.

Irish Man My wife has left me!

JPW I don't care! (*He goes to bed.*)

Irish Man She took my son!

JPW I don't care!

Irish Man Will you listen to me!

JPW She will have returned home before you this afternoon!

Irish Man I don't want her back!

JPW So all is well!

Irish Man I'll never forgive her. She says she's afraid I'll hurt the child. I never hurt her! So how can she say such a thing? I thought I was very well when I left here yesterday.

JPW You were drunk.

Irish Man I thought I was very well last night but it took me by surprise again.

JPW Ben-i-millo!

Irish Man I started shouting. My son, crying, down the stairs, 'She's only trying to help'. She's only trying to help! It was brave of him, brave little boy, yes, but she's only trying to help. She'd went upstairs, haggard face, up to bed, only trying to help me? And I was feeling very well.

JPW You were drunk.

Irish Man Wha'? I *roared* at the child. Obscenities. Brave little boy. But now she'd got her suitcase. And took him with her. His face to the back windscreen, driving away, tears running down his face, waving bye-bye, bye-bye, like a baby. And I just stood there, the lights driving away, don't go, don't go.

JPW You are a terrible drinker. You're *terrible* drinker!

Irish Man Wha'? . . . I told you I was!

JPW Terrible. (*He gets up.*)

Irish Man It's not my problem.

JPW (*sharing the last of a bottle with him*) Well, it is a problem this morning.

Irish Man And I left my Gigli record here with you.

JPW Here, the last hair of the dog.

Irish Man (*takes glass unconsciously*) I wouldn't hurt my child.

JPW Now it is Sunday morning and you arrived – what? – three hours early and great lapsed churchgoing people that we are, half of this city is still sensibly in its bed. But you have got me up and, double-time or not, I want something more for my endeavours, so . . . Yes! Sex, if you please.

Irish Man I don't *think* I would hurt my son. Or her.

JPW I'll give you a kick-off then. My first sexual encounter was in mixed-infants.

Irish Man My wife –

JPW Only matters sexual now or I-shall-not-listen!

A silent contest of wills.

Irish Man . . . Maisie Kennedy.

JPW Yes?

Irish Man She took me to the end of our garden where the potatoes were.

JPW Yes?

Irish Man She, well, then, sort of, took me down on top of her, so that we become hid between the drills, and she kept putting sweets into my mouth while she was trying to get my . . .

JPW You're doing fine.

Irish Man Trying to get my – micky into her.

JPW Yes? (*He goes back to bed.*)

Irish Man I enjoyed the sweets but my micky was too young to repay her treat.

JPW Very good – you see? – you are quite normal.

Irish Man Sex has nothing to do with it!

JPW Don't stop now – let it all come out – Your first time, what was that like?

Irish Man I was twenty-two.

JPW I was twenty-three, clumsy affair – Sorry.

Irish Man I got very excited and I almost ran, hurrying home to tell Danny. Danny was next in age to me, I was the youngest and I think he was always a bit embarrassed by my – innocence, I think. He was asleep, but I was proud of myself and I wanted to tell him so that he'd see I wasn't a fool. And I woke him up and told him I'd – had it. And he just rolled over and said, 'how many times' and went back to sleep. . . . You see, Danny (*'There's a story.'*) . . . You see, my eldest brother had singled out Danny as the one to be put through school, educated. But I don't think school suited our Danny. But I don't think my eldest brother wanted to admit that. But my father, sick, and then dying, and my eldest brother had took over, and he became a sort of tyrant.

JPW That would be Abramo?

Irish Man Mick. Mick frightened us all. Shouting, kicking his bike. Kicking the doors, shouting. My mother thought the world of him. He used to parade his learning too. 'Can anyone tell me what was St Bernadette's second name?' 'Soubrou', or whatever it was. Imagine, he used to give Danny tests. In arithmetic, I suppose. And I'd be sitting quietly, hoping that Danny, locked upstairs in that room, would pass Mick's examination paper . . . And Danny was always trying to teach me – cunning, I think. Street sense. He used to tell me never trust anyone, and that everything is based on hate. He used to tell me that when I got big, if I was ever in a fight with Mick, to watch out, that Mick would use a poker. I suppose he knew he'd never be able for Mick, unless he shot him, or knifed him. But we didn't do things that way . . . I wanted to be a priest. I was crazy, I was thirteen. But some notion in my head about – dedicating? – my life to others. But Mick, in consultation with my mother – and rightly so – said wait a couple of years. And one day – and the couple of years weren't up – and Mick was in a black mood . And he'd beaten Danny that day too for something or other, and I had went outside. Oh, just outside, sitting on the patch of grass. And. There's only two flowers for children from my kind of background. The daisy and the . . . the yellow one.

JPW Primrose.

Irish Man The primrose too – the buttercup. Oh, just sitting there, picking them off the grass. And Mick come out. What about the priesthood, he said. I'd changed my mind but I didn't tell him. I said – I stood up. The couple of years isn't up I said. But he knew I'd changed my mind and he said, you're stupid, and he flattened me. I knew what he was at, I was learning. That day the priesthood would've gave the family a bit of status. But, unfortunately for the family, that day I'd changed my mind . . . Oh yes, the flowers. And. I still had this little bunch of flowers. In my hand. I don't think I gave a fuck about the flowers. A few – daisies, and the – yellow ones. But Danny – he was eighteen! – and he was inside, crying. And it was the only thing I could think of. (*He is only just managing to hold back his tears.*) And. And.

I took the fuckin' flowers to our Danny . . . wherever he is now . . . and I said, which do you think is nicest? The most beautiful, yeh know? And Danny said 'Nicest?', like a knife. 'Nicest? Are you stupid? What use is nicest?' Of what use is beauty, Mr King?

JPW (*gently*) Two million pounds later, Benimillo?

Irish Man Actually, a little more.

JPW James, Jimmy.

Irish Man But I've strayed from your subject, Mr King.

JPW That's okay. Would you like a cup of tea?

Irish Man (*nods 'Yes', then*) In assets. I never keep much cash.

JPW And I bet you had no breakfast. Tck! You need your food. (*He has got up again and put on his trousers.*)

Irish Man I think I should go home. (*But he does not move.*) Do you have brothers and sisters?

JPW No. Just me.

Irish Man And you never went back to see your mother before she died?

JPW Oh, Mama's not dead. She tried to take her life when Father died. She loved him. Though their worlds were worlds apart. But they brought her back. Or she came back. Extraordinary really, because she was always rather delicate. And apparently she was calling my name. Oh! we had a deal – Father and I – which I kept. He promised he would give me five hundred pounds if I did not take a drink until I was twenty-five.

Irish Man Why didn't you go back since?

JPW Not with tail between my legs, Benimillo. What did your brother do, the authoritative one, Mick?

Irish Man Oh, something the equivalent of shovelling shit. (*Laughs harshly, vindictively.*) And it took him forty years to become a clerk!

JPW Let me clear some of these things out of the way. A frustrated young man –

Irish Man He wasn't a young man, he was in his thir – (*Thirties.*) He wasn't a young man.

JPW Do you take sugar? Mick was hardly twenty at the time. There was a fattening bag of 'comelackt shoekree erin' (*Comhlucht Siuicre Eireann, sugar.*) about the place at one point.

Irish Man I don't feel inclined to forgive anyone. And I'll never forgive her for last night.

He continues motionless through the following, all the time faced towards the window or the doorway. **JPW** *preparing tea.*

JPW Kettle? (*Which is in his hand.*) That's the kettle. Water? (*Checks kettle.*) That's water. (*He plugs in the kettle and sits watching it.*) I used to watch my father too, secretly. Pottering with one of the gardeners. Straight back, head bowed, looking at his flowers and vegetables as if he was puzzled by them. I wanted to take his hand. But fathers, you know? Formal, straight backs, frowning, unsure of themselves. I think they feel a little spare, and that is a pity.

Irish Man Did he pay up? Before he died.

JPW Oh yes, always kept his word. I bought my first car with that five hundred. Yes, I think he loved her. And me. And Mama, though I was otherwise engaged when she was calling, would know that I loved her too. Now to wash my best china.

He goes to washroom with two mugs.

Irish Man Sum up?

JPW (*off*) What?

Irish Man (*beginnings of a roar*) Sum up!

JPW (*off*) Oh! I think you are a basso!

Irish Man (*hisses at doorway*) I hate! I f-f-f-f-h-h-h-ate . . .

His hand clutching something in his pocket. A few whimpers escape . . .
fixed, rooted in his position, he starts to shout, savage, inarticulate roars
of impotent hatred at the doorway . . . developing into sobs which he
cannot stop . . . He is on his hands and knees. Terrible dry sobbing, and
rhythmic, as if from the bowels of the earth. **JPW** *emerging, slowly,*
wide-eyed from the washroom. The sobbing continuing.

JPW Yes . . . yes . . . that's it, Benimillo . . . that is what it
is like . . . Let it come out . . . Let it all come out . . . Take
my hand . . . if you so wish to . . . We all love you, Benimillo
. . . Very good . . . That is very good.

Irish Man (*sobs subsiding into tears*) Sorry.

JPW I know.

Irish Man I'm sorry.

JPW I know.

Irish Man I'm sorry.

JPW I know . . . and you are so tired . . . I know.

Irish Man To sing? To sing?

JPW I know. We'll do it.

Irish Man To sing. (*The sobbing finished, tears and laughter. He*
is lying on the bed.)

JPW Goodness gracious! . . . What! . . . Good heavens! I
have never heard such crying! What? Good grief! Dear me!

My word! That was some – what! And the kettle is boiling!
(*Tending to kettle, making tea.*) And we shall have a little
music in a moment. Actually, my worst sexual experience
was not my first one, or second, or third. One of those
half-virgins. A simple soul, God bless her. But she thought
we were destined for the altar and, consequently, she was
covering herself against the possibility of a post-marital attack.
Because she had not been completely *virgo intacta* for me, her
future husband. The stable-boy had got in there when she was
only fourteen she told me. 'I think he half done me,' she said,
'but Daddy caught him.' Caught him where, I wonder? Well,
my girl, I said, now you can feel secure at last in the fact
that you have just been fully done. And I congratulated her
on having received from my good self the official stamp and
approval of A-one fulfilling sexual intercourse. Her simple face
fell. Was that what that was, she said. The startling thing, I
was thirty-one years of age at the time. Left me with a few
complexes for a while, I can tell you. Now, a little music. (*He
switches on the machine: Gigli singing 'Agnus Dei'.*) And the tea
. . . Benimillo? . . . Benimillo?

Irish Man *is asleep on the bed.* **JPW** *covers him with a blanket. Then
he sees* **Irish Man**'s *hat, gets an idea, picks it up, hides it. He sits with
his tea, reading a book. Lights fading to evening light.* **JPW** *switches on
his reading lamp. The end of the 'Agnus Dei' cross-fading into 'Cangia
cangia tu voglie' by Fasola.* **Irish Man** *waking up. A certain disgust
at discovering himself in these surroundings and in* **JPW**'s *bed.*

JPW Awake at last. You needed that sleep . . . Hmm?

Irish Man *asks silently for permission to wash his hands in the
washroom. He exits to washroom.*

Sum up? Or shall I make some fresh tea? . . . The truth is,
we have become fast friends . . . What?

Church clock chiming eight. **Irish Man** *enters. A brief look about for
his hat.*

Tomorrow we start transcending a few things, Tuesday you
sing . . . Your record! You'll need it tonight.

Irish Man *has gone out of door.*

See you tomorrow! . . . Twelve o'clock?

But **Irish Man** *is gone. The four walls, the vodka bottle empty. He considers the phone. Makes usual adjustment to connection-box, then changes his mind about making phonecall (but forgets to make readjustment to the connection-box). He produces* **Irish Man**'s *hat and sits, tie dangling unconsciously from his hand. Gigli sings on, 'Cangia, cangia, tu voglie' to its conclusion.*

Scene Six

Office empty, record-player switched off, church clock chiming twelve. **JPW** *comes hurrying in. He has added the old tie to affect a less casual dress and he is wearing* **Irish Man**'s *hat. He is pleased that he has got back to his office in time and is arranging himself in anticipation of* **Irish Man**'s *call. He switches on the record-player. A paper bag from his pockets and a quarter bottle of vodka . . . waiting . . . loosens his tie . . . has a swig of vodka . . . Looking out of the door, the window . . .*

JPW Benimillo . . . Benimillo . . .

Gigli singing 'Puisqu'on ne peut pas fléchir'. Lights fading.

Scene Seven

Irish Man *arriving angrily.* **JPW** *asleep on the bed.*

Irish Man Mr King! Mr King!

JPW What?

Irish Man Mr King!

JPW Who is that?

Irish Man I'd like to have a word with you.

JPW What time is it?

Irish Man Mr King!

JPW Come in.

Irish Man I'm in! (*He switches off the machine.*)

JPW (*fully awake*) Benimillo! Come in, my friend, sit down!

Irish Man I'll stand if you don't mind.

JPW Benimillo!

Irish Man Mr King –

JPW Have I got stories for you, have I got the goodies for you!

Irish Man Mr King! –

JPW You never let me get a word in edgeways!

Irish Man Mr King, this has gone on too long. But before I go into that, I'd like to say something about yesterday.

JPW What day is today?

Irish Man You may think you can read my mind, well, you can't.

JPW What?

Irish Man Better men have tried and failed. Bigger men and better games than this – or trying to influence me with trickster stuff, hypnosis and the likes, I suppose – well, you can't. I'd lose you and find you. I know what you've been up to.

JPW Oh, yesterday! I shouldn't feel embarrassed about yesterday.

Irish Man I'm not – Do I look embarrassed to you?

JPW Emotional incontinence. People break down here all the time, my friend.

Irish Man Who broke down?

JPW Curley Wee then perhaps?

Irish Man Oh yes, cheap cracks, jokes –

JPW I thought we had a terrific day yesterday!

Irish Man Listen, I'd just like you to know for one thing, boy, that I had a very happy childhood, you'd like to suggest otherwise, but I'm up to you. Deprived of my father, yes, but my mother, my mother, the Lord have mercy on her, *liked* my father very much, and I often seen her crying. Often, she'd tell me, tears in her eyes, how my father was good to his mother when his mother was old and decrepit, tears in her eyes – that my father slept in the same room – the same bed! – as his mother to nurse and look after her every need. Tears in my mother's eyes telling me that, boy. And Mick – Mick! – Often he'd give me a penny of a Friday to go out and buy a copy-book for myself out of his six-shilling pay-packet and the rest to my mother. Oh, but, five hundred pounds to buy a motor car! And crashed it, I suppose! Your breed would laugh at a six-shilling pay-packet, let alone a penny! I just thought I'd let you know, A very happy childhood.

JPW That's good. You are already on to the next stage, transcending, celebrating the past. (*Offering him a drink.*)

Irish Man Celebrating the – No, I don't want your drink – and then on to dirty stories and then pumping me for more information. And Mick – Mick! – Mick was a good singer – when he wanted to. 'The Snowy-breasted Pearl', boy. Thought I'd let you know.

JPW Did your wife return?

Irish Man What! What! Is that any business of yours? Wasting my time and my money as if it grew on the trees. I should have done it myself like I always done. But what a fool, I came to you. Why are you smiling?

JPW I'm not. (*But he is inclined to laugh.*)

Irish Man Mr King – Mr King! You done nothing. Now I think I deserve something more for my time and money. Before I go, is-there-anything-you-can-tell-me? Why are you laughing? . . . You're laughing because you don't know or there's something funny?

JPW I thought you weren't going to show up!

Irish Man That's all you can say?

JPW Well, has anyone told you you look twenty years younger since you started coming to me?

Irish Man They haven't. Anything else?

JPW Well, you do.

Irish Man And that's it? Pathetic. I told you at the start I have little or no time for psychiatrists, now I have none whatsoever for quacks. And, yes, my wife is back. And, yes, I made my first attempt for months to make conversation with her at lunchtime. I told her I was simply bored to distraction: she took it as a reflection on herself and left the room in tears. You're not able to explain that either, I suppose? I left her there – why wouldn't I? – and drove out into the country for myself, the first time in months, beautiful nature all around me, fine sites for development. Will I build a thousand more? No, I've made up my mind on that one. There's more to life than working myself to death or wheeling and dealing with that criminal band of would-be present-day little pigmy Napoleons we've got at the top. Let them have the profit. I need a breath of fresh air. Stopped the car to get out and my only other last hat blew away – (*Sees his hat.*) – Jesus, there's the other one! Well fuck the fuckin' hats! (*He throws the hat from him.*)

JPW Bis! Bis!

Irish Man What? Hah?

JPW I did not expect it until tomorrow, but not quite
Gigli yet.

Irish Man Look, Mr King, be warned. I could have you locked
up, like that, one telephone call. But why go throwing good
money after bad. And it was my own fault. I just can't get
over what possessed me to come into a place like this when
I can cure myself like I did last time.

JPW Last time?

Irish Man *And* the time before that!

JPW How often do you get depressed? Unhappy.

Irish Man Not that it's any of your business, but smart man
that you think you are and because I can do what you can't,
I'll tell you. Once every year or two. Last time I just went
away and hid in a corner – you learn a lot from animals –
like a dog in a corner, you couldn't prise me out of it, and
stayed there licking my wounds till I cured myself.

JPW You should have told me.

Irish Man The time before, boy, I went into your territory,
debauchery, Mr King: got a dose of the clap in the course of
the treatment, but I cured myself.

JPW And the next time?

Irish Man I'm looking forward to it already!

JPW You should have told me.

Irish Man About what?

JPW The pattern!

Irish Man That would have made all the difference, would
it?

JPW You told me you wanted to *sing*.

Irish Man I did. The other times I wanted to do other things.

JPW Tap-dancing?

Irish Man *laughs at him.*

And I told someone this morning that this was a once-off do-or-die aspiration, that there was no pattern – because that is what you told me! – and how astonishing it would be to achieve it.

Irish Man And so much for your confidentiality, hah?

JPW I'd be wary of the next one, Benimillo.

Irish Man I must remember that. Charlatan, quack, parasite! And, yeh know, there's a stink in this pig-sty: you'd be better off cleaning it up. Sum up?

JPW . . . Yes. Last year, ladies, debauchery and the clap, this year, grand opera and me. And I done nothing? (*Producing books from various places.*) Here, these are yours. Kierkegaard, you read it, make sense of it, stolen out of the South Side Library. Here, Jung, Freud, Otto Rank, Ernest Becker, Stanislav Grof, anonymous donations to your cause, courtesy of Eason's, Greene's – Trinity College! Heidegger, try sitting up all night with him for jolly company. What's this? No, you have this one already, *Memoirs of Beniamino Gigli* – Ida treated him badly all right. Wait! (*He slams the door shut.*) This is your property, you hired me to procure it and there is not a decent library or bookshop in Dublin that I have not shadily visited to get it for you. I'm summing up, it's my turn, and it is only fair.

Do you know, Benimillo, how hard it is to get an appointment with a psychiatrist at short notice? I managed two this morning. I, as you, arrived early for one appointment and saw the chief himself going into his office. I slipped in after him, wearing your hat, my hand in my pocket – like you do it. The chief thought he was in for it! I dropped to my knees, my hands in the air, to reassure him. I said I wanted to sing like Gigli, my father was a cobbler, bis-bis-bis, can you help me? The chief, in a whisper, 'Just a mo. Excuse.' Luckily I went to the keyhole, he was rounding up his men and deputing others to prepare a padded cell. They nearly nabbed me. Out the front door, in the back, met by the pursuing posse, out again, three times round the garden, hid in a bush, the berberis family – look at the scratches! Until I figured they had figured I had escaped. But I had to get in there again, an official appointment for a quarter to ten. Could not risk the front door, or the back, so what was there to do! In through the window of the waiting room. Two waiting patients left – cured. Sweated it out behind the *Beano* until I was called to the third-assistant psychiatrist's office where I – you – Mickeleen O'Loughlin had an appointment.

The psychiatrist was a lady, in years just a little over-ripe, but that was the last thing on my mind. I want to sing like Gigli, I was born in Recanati, bis-bis-bis, can you help me? Was I homosexual? I told her about Ida. Was I *sure* I was not homosexual? She had at this stage taken off her not-very-sensible shoes for-a-lady-of-her-years under the desk, and was now removing her spectacles to suck them slyly sideways. 'Tell me, Mr O'Loughlin, what do you expect of me?' she said softly. I misinterpreted – I was losing my nerve: I told her I thought she was beautiful. No, she said, did I expect medication, analysis or therapy from her. Could I have a glass of water and an aspirin, please, I said, and while I had her occupied, I was stealing the six sheets that I now needed from her prescription pad. Goodness knows what the aspirin was, I have not been feeling well all day. But I took it – loudly! – demonstrating my great preference above all else for medication. Because we, Benimillo, had been most remiss, neglecting so completely to enlist the power of medication to sing like Gigli, and I set to pumping her on the subject. Oh, and do you know her fees? Thirty pounds! – Hmmm? – For twenty-five minutes! I thought it was all for free! Cheque or cash? Send the bill, I said. Gave my correct address too – I just could not think fast enough: the surprise that one could make enormous fortunes at this game, plus the further complication, the chief's voice once more in the hall: he was now calming down his men, and they were nearly back to normal. But I could not risk it: they are most dedicated people, and I did not have the further strength to run if they got excited again. So, thank you, to the good lady, and excuse, as I slipped out to the rose-garden through *her* window.

Irish Man I'm sorry.

JPW Not at all.

Irish Man I'm –

JPW Not at all.

Irish Man I didn't think –

JPW All part of the service.

Irish Man I'll call you tomorrow.

JPW No tomorrow.

Irish Man I didn't mean –

JPW You did mean! I-have-not-finished! You did mean. And you are quite right. Here, these, also, are for you – (*The small paper bag he returned with.*) Sweeties, on forged prescriptions. Insidon, anti-downers, one three times daily will get you to a high C. If you should find that they do not get you through the day singing – where's my topper-up? – Here, Nobrium – Excellent name for this kind of stuff whoever thought it up. And what are these? – Here – No, these are for myself: Frisium, to put bounce back into my hair (*He takes some.*) – and to tranquillise my nerves. Sorry, but I really need these because I have not had a moment's peace or a decent hour's sleep since I clapped eyes on you.

Irish Man Jimmy.

JPW No! You did mean! And you are quite right to walk in here four hours late. It is a pig-sty, I am a charlatan and a quack, and I have *never* achieved *anything* in my life! And stupid, you left out that one. I even learned the baritone role of the duet on that thing – and I am the *tenor*! – thought we might give it a whirl together tomorrow. *I-am-the-tenor!*

Irish Man I spoke out of turn.

JPW And that gun that you have been terrifying me with.

Irish Man What gun?

JPW And I am sure there will be a warrant out for my arrest.

Irish Man What gun?

JPW Your trump card, the final word, that gun in your pocket that you have been threatening to shoot yourself with, or me – I never knew which.

Irish Man These? (*He produces a small cylindrical container of pills.*) Mandrax, sleeping pills. (*He dumps them in the waste-paper basket.*)

JPW . . . Do you think you have *got* me then?

Irish Man No.

JPW Do you think you have won?

Irish Man No. No.

JPW Well, you have not! Have you seen it through?

Irish Man I'll call –

JPW Is this what you call seeing it through?

Irish Man I'll call and see you –

JPW Well, you have not!

Irish Man When you have cooled down.

JPW You have not!

Irish Man When you have –

JPW Rather not. No! . . . No.

Irish Man *goes out.*

You have not won, Benimillo. I have not finished.

He switches on record-player. Gigli singing 'Tu che a Dio spiegasti l'ali' from 'Lucia De Lammermoor', with bass and chorus. He emits a few pitiful howls in attempt at singing. The telephone rings. He approaches it cautiously, like a man approaching a trap and lifts the receiver.

Hello? . . . Hello? . . . Who? . . . Helen? . . . Helen! Are you still there? . . . Fine . . . I have been very fine. (*Silently, 'Helen!'*) . . . No, I'm still here. I just cannot, I mean to say – Helen! . . . What? . . . Music. Beniamino Gigli . . . You've heard of him? Really? (*Celebratory laugh.*) Born in Bunratty! (or, Killarney) . . . No, I'm laughing because, I mean to say – how are you? . . . What is the matter? . . . Why are you crying? . . . Why are you . . . Pardon? . . . I did not phone you yesterday because . . . I did not phone you the day before because . . . You asked me not to. To promise, not to call you. What? . . . (*Shocked.*) I am a *what*? . . . Dirty? I never made a dirty phonecall to you . . . And if I ever call you again you shall . . . Send the police! . . . Hello? . . . Hello? (*He puts down the phone.*) Bloody hell.

He is stunned . . . He remembers the Mandrax and is on his hands and knees searching the waste-paper basket for them. **Mona** *arrives.*

Mona Well, lover! Some batteries for your shaver and a present.

She puts batteries, a pot plant and a bottle of vodka on the desk and she leaves an overnight bag which she is carrying somewhere. She goes to the record-player.

What's this?

JPW (*absently*) I am very busy right now, Mona. Bloody hell. (*He finds the container of Mandrax; he is half-frightened of them, then becoming conscious of* **Mona**, *and relieved by her presence.*

He puts the Mandrax in his pocket.) Mona! You would not believe it, people are crazy! You are the absolutely only normal human being in the world!

He has come up behind her and circled her waist with his arms. She likes the feeling of his arms around her but the cloud of her secret sadness is moving across her face.

And how is Karen-Marie, your god-child?

Mona What god-child?

JPW (*not listening*) Isn't that interesting?

She is turning away in the direction of the bed, the music cross-fading from 'Tu che a Dio spiegasti l'ali' to 'Caro mio ben', leading into the final scene.

Scene Eight

JPW and **Mona** *dressed as before –* **Mona** *minus her overcoat and gloves – lying on the bed, something childlike about them, huddled together, eyes on the record-player, listening to the music. Gigli singing 'Caro mio ben' followed by 'Amarilli'.*

Mona That's the fourth – fifth? – time round. You could go away for a year with that thing switched on and it would still be playing when you got back.

JPW Yeh.

Mona How many were singing in the last one?

JPW The sextet?

Mona I like that best.

JPW Yeh.

Mona How many were singing in it?

JPW The sextet? Three.

Mona What's he singing, what's he saying now?

JPW You don't have to know, whatever you like.

Mona Beloved.

JPW If you like.

Mona That everything ends.

JPW Yes. But that at least we end up friends. At least that.

Mona That everything ends anyway. And does it matter –
does-it-matter! – if it all ends now, a few seconds earlier, for
God's sake! . . . Jimmy.

*He offers her the bottle of vodka absently. She declines. She looks at
her watch.*

JPW That you are breathing, now, this moment . . . alive in
Time at the same time as I . . . and that I can only hold my
breath at the thought.

Mona That's nice.

JPW Beloved.

Mona Why don't you call me that? . . . There's someone or
something wounding you very deeply, and I can't do a thing
about it.

JPW (*a new thought*) No. That is what I *used* to think.
(*Offering her the bottle again.*) *You* and I are alive in Time
at the same time.

Mona I'm not meant to. (*Then she changes her mind, a silent
'fuck it' and she takes a swig.*) Why do you put up with it?

JPW You're not listening to me.

Mona When life is –

JPW (*celebratory laugh*) Bouncing back! Isn't that interesting!
Bother the lot of them.

Mona When life is short. And *I'm* here. Well – (*About to qualify the last, changes her mind.*) Some bird you want to screw, is it? I'd do that for you in a wheelchair on the fucking moon. The way some of you mope about. I know you think I'm vulgar.

JPW No. I think you are –

Mona Well, I am not. Oh fuck it, maybe I am. But all our family is! Brothers, sisters, Mammy, Daddy – ten of us! – You should hear us all together! – We're all vulgar! But the way I look at things, if life is, as they say, just a preparation for heaven, then what's the big deal about life about?

JPW What are you talking about?

Mona But if there is no heaven, what's the big deal about heaven about? So, I say, make the most of what's available now, grab what you can.

JPW *opens his mouth to speak.*

Yes, pleasure too, but I mean even more. All that energy about. Why are people moping? All that energy in the world, to be enjoyed, to kill pain, to give to the children.

JPW What's wrong?

Mona (*she has another long swig of vodka*) And watch them grow up.

JPW You are not listening.

Mona . . . I'm listening to you. (*Her eyes on the machine.*) Do you know what he's (*Gigli.*) saying? A baby. That's what it's all about.

JPW The farmer's wife! (*He is looking at her intently, seeing her potential.*) And a lot of easy money to be made in farming. I could be a farmer.

Mona *laughs.*

Well, it's possible.

Mona That's what you said to me in the supermarket, anything is possible.

JPW We are a very good team, Mona.

Mona Too late.

JPW Hmmm?

Mona You wouldn't be able to buy a farm now anyway. Why didn't you invest your money?

JPW Yes, well, but. I'm glad you're here.

Mona I know. I feel it for the first time.

JPW Do you? (*'Isn't that interesting?'*) What are you looking at your watch for?

Mona I wasn't. I got a letter from my young sister today, do you want to hear?

JPW Yes. Bother the lot of them. (*He switches off the machine.*) And if he comes back for that (*Machine.*) I'll have it hocked, tell him it was stolen.

Mona Here's a bit. This is the hospital where she works and there's this young doctor, and he was passing remarks about 'the pips' under Caroline's uniform. All of us are like that too, up here. (*Small-breasted.*) The girls, that is, (*Reading.*) '. . . the pips under my uniform and I said you wouldn't like one of them up your arse as a pile, would you. So the laugh was on him.' I told you! We all talk like that. (*Suddenly grave.*) But you should see our Caroline. She's beautiful.

JPW Like you.

Mona 'Daddy made custard two nights ago and, mind you, it was very nice. So he made it again last night. It was like soup, all lumpy, and no one could eat it. So we gave it to the dogs. All the dogs had their feet in the air in the morning.' It's nice to get a letter when you're not expecting it. But I can see them there, all together, with Daddy's custard. Jimmy, I have cancer. I've been going to doctors for another purpose, but life is full of surprises.

JPW Breast cancer? (*Motionless – and continues so through the following.*)

Mona Tck, no! You should know that. Glands, lymphs. I wanted to lie beside you for a while. I've been delaying. I've to go in a minute.

JPW The lymphatic system?

Mona Yeh. I go in tonight to start the treatment, nip it in the bud. My husband – honestly, that man! – started crying when I told him. Silly c – sorry – clunt. Oh for God's sake, I said, I'm Not-Dead-Yet! (*Aside to him.*) Hard to kill a bad thing. Will you send me flowers?

JPW New cures all the time.

Mona Yes! – that's what I told him! – Wonder drugs! And, if the worst comes to the worst, as they say – (*A movement to restrain her from getting up.*) I have to go, Jimmy – I have no regrets. (*Dressing, overcoat, gloves through the following.*) Well, a few. I had a little girl when I was sixteen. They didn't mean to, but now I know they pressurised me. They wanted the father's name. I wouldn't give it. They needed it to have her adopted. I wouldn't give it. Still, they had her adopted some way. Things hadn't gone right, complications, and I was very ill. I only saw her twice. She was so tiny. She's twenty-two now. Somewhere. I've been trying to repeat the deed ever since. I picked you up. And if I had had a child by you, or any of the others, I don't think I would have told you. I'd have been the one you wouldn't have seen for dust. Pregnant into the sunset. But preferably by you. Others weren't so gentle in how they – regarded me. But it couldn't be done. And maybe just as well now. So I invented a modest god-child, in some kind of – fancy? – in the meantime, to keep me going. But. Karen-Marie. Yeh. Maybe just as well now. Well, my magician friend, am I forgetting anything? (*An imperative:*) Water that. (*The potted plant.*) See yeh.

He nods.

Beloved?

He nods.

I love you.

*She leaves. He switches on the record-player, blasting up the volume –
Elizabeth Rethberg/Gigli/Pinza singing the trio 'Tu sol quest anima'
from 'Attila'. He is now crying, shouting at the door.*

JPW I love! I love you! Fuck you! I love! Fuck you! I love! –
I love! Fuck you – fuck you! I love . . .

Gigli's voice now taking over from Rethberg's and **JPW** *appears to be
finding a purpose out of the blaring singing. He remembers the container
of Mandrax in his pocket and he takes a couple, does not like the taste
and washes them down with a swig of vodka. A sudden stomach cramp
but he recovers quickly.*

Silhouette of **Irish Man** *arriving.* **JPW** *does not hear him come in.*
Irish Man *entering – his entrance timed with bass solo in the trio
from 'Attila'. He is dressed in tuxedo, smoking a cigar, has had a few
drinks; beaming. He is unsure about* **JPW**'s *attitude, whether or not it
is to be taken as banter. He has a present of a bottle of vodka. His first
lines are spoken under the music.* **JPW**, *in half doubled-up position,
continues motionless for some time.*

Irish Man Can I come in? I drank you out of house and home
the other day. I was a bit shy, hesitating about calling. Can
we have a little one together? Will I open this, or – (*He takes
the bottle already opened.*) Waste not, want not, and you'll have
a little store in for yourself. (*He puts a drink in* **JPW**'s *hand,
then switches off the music.*) Aa, the aul' music! The itinerants
moved on. Oh, d'yeh mind? (*The cigar.*) They moved on,
the creatures. It cost me a few bob but – ah, my place wasn't
a suitable place at all for them. Please God they'll find a more
suitable site. They have a tough life of it and it's not their
fault. (*He sits.*) Oh, d'yeh mind? Just for a minute. But I
was doing my sums going home in the car and it come into
my head. Supposing my life depended on it, who would I turn

to? I went through mothers, brothers, relations. The wife. It all boils down to the wife for us all in the end. So we're going out for the evening. I left her (*Down the road.*) with some friends for a few minutes. Good luck, God bless, cheers! And I couldn't help thinking – Hah-haa, you're a queer one! – strange as the route you took me, you had some kind of hand in leading me to that conclusion.

JPW It is Tuesday?

Irish Man No. What?

JPW Final session.

Irish Man (*laughs*) Aw!

JPW A refund?

Irish Man (*laughs*) No!

JPW But the job is not finished.

Irish Man I'm fine – thanks in some measure to you.

JPW But it can be done. To sing. The sound to clothe our emotion and aspiration. And what an achievement.

Irish Man The next one, the one you warned me about.

JPW No, we have tried laughing, and crying, and philosophy.

Irish Man You're a case!

JPW I have boiled it down to two options. Have you considered surgery?

Irish Man An operation is it?

JPW (*laughing – but quite likely precipitated by a stomach cramp*) You were taking me seriously there. (*Offering to top up his drink.*)

Irish Man No – no – no! I don't know how to take you, Mr King.

JPW And naughty Benimillo, you have a few in you already.

Irish Man And by the looks of you, you've had more than your share. I'd a drop of champagne. Champagne is light d'yeh know. Was I your first client?

JPW (*absently; looking out of window or door*) No. There was one other. It's pretty bad out there, isn't it?

Irish Man Oh, now.

JPW Ever returning, waking up, lying down, more unhappy.

Irish Man You can surprise yourself and find yourself strayed too far from the world all right . . . You're looking very pale.

JPW So I bring my last option into play. Have you considered magic?

Irish Man Mr King –

JPW You are going to ask me what is magic –

Irish Man Mr King, Mr King!

JPW Jimmy! Jimmy!

Irish Man Jimmy. Jimmy. And we are friends, and I'm sorry I upset you today, and I'm sorry I have to rush now, but I called because I was wondering if there was some way I could repay all the trouble you took. If there was some way at all?

JPW It is rest for me to take trouble for a friend.

Irish Man That's it, that's –

JPW Persian proverb.

Irish Man That's the kind you are but, reality, face the facts. And I'm not talking a hundred or two hundred. A couple of grand, to set you up. You did a great job.

JPW No, not yet.

Irish Man I could stretch it to three.

JPW I shan't hold you. I know you have to rush – And don't tell me: you are going on a holiday? I knew it. These little ceremonies can be pleasantly tranquillising. You have taken yourself captive again, but dread still lies nesting, Benimillo.

Irish Man (*preparing to go*) Well, I'm very grateful to you.

JPW No, I am grateful to you. I longed to take myself captive too and root myself, but you came in that door with the audacity of despair, wild with the idea of wanting to soar, and I was the most pitiful of spiritless things.

Irish Man Well.

JPW Leave it to me, Benimillo.

Irish Man And I did get the right man for the job.

JPW Oh, and your machine!

Irish Man No, you keep that.

JPW (*logically*) But I shan't require it.

Irish Man Since you'll take nothing else. No, a little gift . . . Go home, Jimmy. Forget that – Irish colleen. You *are* a remarkable man. I know there's kindness in the world, but they'll kill you over here. (*Silently.*) Go home.

*He leaves. **JPW** into action. He locks the door, switches off the record-player, unplugs it from its power-point as a double precaution (and proof). He looks out of the window for a moment, then draws the blind. He goes to his desk where he spreads jam on a slice of bread, cuts the bread into squares and decorates each square with a Mandrax pill. Through the following, a red glow, as if emanating from the reading lamp with the red shade, suffuses the room, and the shaft of yellow light from the washroom becoming more intense.*

JPW You are going to ask me what is magic. In a nutshell, the rearrangement and redirection of the orbits and trajectories of dynamatological whirlings, i.e., simply new mind over old matter. This night I'll conjure. If man can bend a spoon with beady steadfast eye, I'll sing like Gigli or I'll die. Checklist. Too many facts in the world. Addiction to those lies arrested. Rationalisations recognised – yes, you have dallied too long with your destiny. All alibis exhausted, desire for achievement, mind set on goal. Trump card – (*He pops a square of bread and jam with pill on top into his mouth and washes it down with vodka.*) And wait. (*After a moment, he opens his mouth as if to sing. An abortive sound/silence. Another piece of bread and jam with pill on top* . . .)And wait, wait, wait . . . until the silence is pregnant with the tone urgent to be born . . . The soul! Of course! The soul of the singer is the subconscious self. Realistic thinking, honest desire for assistance. (*To heaven.*) Rather not. You cut your losses on this little utopia of greed and carnage some time ago, my not so very clever friend. (*To the floor.*) Assist please. In exchange – (*Another square of bread and jam with pill into his mouth and washes it down with vodka. Faintly – and as on echo, from a distance – orchestral introduction for the aria 'Tu che a Dio spiegasti l'ali'. Whispers:*) What? Yesss! Thank you. But just a mo. (*Gestures, cueing out music, takes another pill, and decides against further vodka.*) Stops taking alcohol, purity of potion, contentment in abstinence, care of personal appearance, diminishing fears of unknown future, resolution fixed in mind for possibilising it, increase in control to achieve it. (*Orchestral introduction begins again.*) Abyss sighted! All my worldly goods I leave to nuns. Leeep! (*Leap.*) pluh-unnge! (*Plunge. And a sigh of relief.*) Aah! Rebirth of ideals, return of self-esteem, future known.

On cue, he sings the aria to its conclusion – Gigli's voice; the recording he made solo, without bass and chorus. The glow of red light receding, as to its point of origin (the small reading lamp) and shaft of yellow light becoming less intense: lights back to normal. **JPW** *on the floor, on hands or knees or whatever, eyes haunted, pained, hurt, frightened. The church clock chiming six am.*

JPW Mama? Mama? Do not leave me in this dark.

Some resilience within pulling himself up . . . He lets up the blind. Early morning light filtering into the room. He looks ghastly. He wonders if he is not dead: a single gasp or grunt to check on this. He remembers record-player: checks to find that it is indeed disconnected from its power-point: smile, laugh of achievement on his face. He puts a few things in an old leather bag and whatever vodka remains into his pocket. He is about to leave, gets an idea. He opens the lower half of his window, plugs in the record-player, switches it on, presses repeat button, 'invites' the music towards the open window. Gigli's 'O Paradiso'.

JPW Do not mind the pig-sty, Benimillo . . . mankind still has a delicate ear . . . that's it . . . that's it . . . sing on forever . . . that's it.

He unlocks the door and goes out, a little unsteady on his feet.